STANGROUND BOY

Yesterday in poems

by
Brian Holdich

By the same author

My Indian Journey
India Revisited
The 2001 New York City Marathon

Published in Great Britain
Brian's Books (B.W. Holdich),
4 Elm Close,
Market Deeping,
Lincs.
PE6 8JN

ISBN 0-9521017-3-4 (Paperback)
Stanground Boy

Printed and bound by Peter Spiegl & Co.,
42 Guash Way, Ryhall Road Industrial Estate,
Stamford, Lincs. PE9 1XH

Foreword

For many of us when we look back across the years there is a period of time that we recall above all others – a period in which the people and events affected us so deeply that it remains in the forefront of our memory for the rest of our lives.

For myself, that period was the eight years between 1939 and 1947 when, as an evacuee from London, I was fostered by the author's parents, Tom and Edna Holdich who, despite having four sons of their own, readily accepted me into their family.

With only two years difference in age between us, it was inevitable that Brian and I would come to spend much of our boyhood together and, because of that, I have fond memories of many of the people and events described in this narrative.

Brian's book is a fascinating portrait of his boyhood after and during the war years and an evocation of village life that had at its centre the all-embracing influence of the church.

Tribute must be paid to the enormous amount of research and hard work that Brian has put into producing this book and it is to be hoped that it will be read by the present generation of children who will obtain from it an insight into village and family life as it was when Brian was growing up. And of course his experiences at Stamford School are most graphic.

With the expansion of Peterborough and the surrounding villages during the last thirty years or so, the Stanground of today is, I believe, very different to what it was during our boyhood and we must be grateful to people like Brian who have recorded for posterity their recollections of a happy and eventful boyhood where the field, the lane and the river were our playground.

Derek A Bishop
Bedfordshire

*In memory of my mother and father and Michael my brother,
as these three are remembered above all others.*

Acknowledgements

With the writing of this book of poems much research has been done in its production, and I feel I must acknowledge certain individuals who have been so supporting of my endeavours.

It has been my privilege to renew acquaintances with friends going back to school days, where there contribution has been invaluable over some problem I was unable to find an answer for, my appreciation therefore goes to, Lol Ayres, Edna Baker, Derek Bishop who kindly wrote the forward to this book, Bill Brewster, John Craddock, (Stamford School Archives), Colin Francis, Keith Gowthorpe, Pam Maycock, Brenda Popkins, Emily Smith, M.J.K. Smith, Cliff Sneesby, Ray Woods, and the staff of the Peterborough library whose help was considerable as I looked through their archives.

Index

Foreword
Acknowledgements
Introduction

Introduction

Why should I write an autobiography in poems of the first fifteen years of my life? Surely only showbiz personalities, celebrities, politicians or famous sports stars would ever qualify to attempt such a task, so why me? And who would ever want to read it anyway? Well, being the author of three books where I've written on subjects so diverse as India and New York, I believe the time is now right for me to write about something nearer home. So what better than to go down Memory Lane and write about my early beginnings, as I have memories galore to be released as I reminisce about my developing years.

Now I know one's life starts immediately when one is born but none of us know much about our lives until we reach the age of about four years old, so it was probably soon after this age that I began to get my very first recollections of my birthplace. But I was to have the greatest of good fortune possible to be born where I was where, incidentally, through the flick of a coin or whatever I came up trumps as my big slice of luck was to be born South of the River Nene and where the river bends.

In this introduction to my "Stanground Boy" book of poems I must emphasize that this book is not just about Stanground as it would be a misconception of the truth if I was to say otherwise as my book also takes into account the three years I attended Stamford School from the age of twelve to fifteen, where the "Stanground Boy" would learn the harsh realities of the discipline of a public school. So this book is not all about Stanground but Mr Bill Brewster, formerly of Stanground, is the only author I know who has written solely about the village which he did in his excellent book called "Stanground: A History" and was published in 1990. Having met Mr Brewster recently, I was keen to assure him that my book would not be a replica of his book as mine would be very different and written in a more personal and intimate way.

Having never published anything in poems before I have to admit it has been a challenge and only from sheer obstinacy and persistence was I able to finish it, as the constant headache of trying to rhyme a line with the previous line was all-time consuming which I never envisaged when I took it upon myself to write in a different way. But putting my poems together has quite astounded me that my memory is still good because I've had to delve deep into my inner self repeatedly and come up with some anecdote that I'd completely forgotten about, which in all probability was lying dormant in my brain somewhere only to be brought back to life again.

This has really surprised me and through long periods of meditation my brain, I'm pleased to say, is in good working order. So in this respect I'm most fortunate that I've been able to put pen to paper and write down my early yesterdays before all is lost. I am most grateful for this.

Undoubtedly some of my very first memories of my life were when war was declared with Germany in 1939 and how it affected life in Stanground during the dark days of that war. As I progressed to an older age, I quickly heard such talk of ration books, gas masks, air-raid shelters, air-raid sirens, shortages of coal and German bombers, which would fly over Peterborough to bomb cities like Coventry we were told. Never far from people's thoughts would be the hardship and poverty of every day life and in my poems I try to give a fair indication of the poverty there was in my home village where recollections of those days never leave me. It was also a period of London children, known as evacuees, who poured out of London in their thousands to live in the provinces. This situation came about because of the fear of London being excessively bombed as the war progressed further. So my parents volunteered to take an evacuee into their home. He became such a part of the family that he stayed for eight years. Stanground had its share of young men being called up for war just like elsewhere and some never did return. Tony, my eldest brother, was called to the Forces and the relief when he came home after the war was considerable. Yet amongst the uncertainty of the horrors of war, I can distinctively remember the wonderful comradeship of everyone in Stanground pulling together. I don't think there could ever have been a time when people were so caring to each other and 'love thy neighbour' was very evident. Then to everyone's delight, the war after nearly six years was over and the memory of V.E. Day and the street parties was done on a grand scale, there being mass celebrations throughout the country with people going wildly ecstatic is something that will live on in my life time.

Yet I think growing up in Stanground while the war was on, I believe I can speak for lots of children at that time that we were not unduly aware of the war or poverty. Providing we had food and a home we couldn't have asked for too much more and even for many years after the war when things generally were not good as the country got back to normality. I did my share of scrumping apples, climbing the highest trees, playing conkers and trying to stay clear of any trouble. It was sport, however, that occupied and played such a pivotal role in my early life and much to the detriment of my schoolwork. Looking back now all I ever wanted to do was play sports, so being such a poor scholar it was no surprise that I failed the 11+. It was then that my parents gave me a marvellous opportunity of a Public School education at Stamford School and it was at this school that my class work deteriorated even more, where any confidence and self-esteem I had left had been eroded from me completely. But the sport at this school was quite fantastic and came to my rescue and made life more bearable. I knew that at sport I could at least compete whereas in the classroom I was a miserable failure. Yet it's strange that despite my problems at Stamford School I have no regrets about ever attending there and wouldn't have missed such an experience, good or bad.

The good being the many sports and friendships made.
The bad being the punishment beatings to amend my ways.

With this introduction to my book, I hope that some of the landmarks mentioned amid many memories will perhaps coincide with recollections others may have of those far off distant days. For me now to reflect on my early life, it has been like an exciting adventure going down my particular memory lane. Memories of the street where I lived with my family are really too numerous for even me to contemplate writing about but I hope these poems portray them with the genuine affection that I have not only for my parents but my brothers too.

Memories of Stanground in wartime are coincided with the inspiring and incomparable speeches of Winston Churchill over a crackling wireless. I well remember American GI's cruising around Stanground in their big American cars. They courted local girls and some became GI brides. The friendly village Bobby is not forgotten and leads me to speculate if only we had that type of policeman today. My memory extends to the boatyards, the Black Bridge, Chapel Street School, Stanground Feast, the Parish Church, the Magnificent Seven and much more. The floods of 1947 will never be allowed to disintegrate from my mind in view of its vastness. I also reminisce about my sporting heroes, which includes the footballers of the Posh going back to 1946, and Stanground Sports Cricket Club players, heroes all. But it was at Stamford School that I saw a real live walking hero who I could see most days, being just two years older than me, who captivated the whole school as a truly outstanding schoolboy cricketer and rugby player. Years later he became an England Cricket Captain and a Double International whom I was to meet 57 years later after first seeing him.

The total number of poems listed is 70 which I hope are well documented and enjoyed. The photographs I have managed to obtain are mostly the late 1940's with the odd one in the 1930's. Others are as recent as 2004. So with being so painstakingly slow with this short book of poems I hope my patience has been rewarded with everything now in place. As I finish this introduction, I further admit to being quite emotionally involved with so much nostalgia along the way. I continue to think with more than a tinge of sadness of the many people who have since departed from this world who subsequently played such a major role in this particular Stanground boy's life all those years ago.

"The success of the poem is determined not by how much the poet felt in writing it -
    But by how much the reader feels in reading it."

John Ciardi

YESTERDAY

Yesterday written by Lennon and McCartney was an absolute classic
    And with my yesterdays much of my childhood is still graphic.
Looking back over the early part of my life it seems only yesterday
    But any troubles I may have had in those years now seem far away.
But yesterday which is always behind us is where I'm going to start
    Because the dear old Stanground I knew really did have a big heart.
There were five streets, one road and a place called Mount Pleasant
    And in Stanground's green fields one might well catch a pheasant.
Church Street is where one finds the St John the Baptist Church
    It stands above all it surveys so there's never a need to search.
North Street, the home of the boatyards, has prolonged seafaring ties
    This being the area where men had very understanding wives.
Chapel Street had its chapel (now a church) and also the senior school
    It was here I realised I'd never be an academic and felt a fool.
South Street with its Police Station is where some went who misbehaved
    Opposite was "The Golden Lion" as drinkers might not act their age.
High Street being a main road which eventually joined up to Fletton
    As floods split the two villages, which some thought was heaven.
Coneygree Road ran into a field and residing there were the gypsies
    They lived in their colourful caravans and I never did see one tipsy.
Mount Pleasant is where a German bomber dropped a bomb in the park
    The noise was earth-shattering, proving too much on the heart.
Stanground in the thirties and forties was about 1,000 in population
    It stayed that way for years, there being very few alterations.
This then is how I remember that village during my formative years
    With many characters and far too many for me to mention here.

A SHORT HISTORY

Stanground has had many earlier names with quite a strong Russian flavour
    As Stangrund, Stangrun and Standground were not names to savour.
These then were Stanground's early names which stretch back to 956
    When the village was first recorded in the Domesday Book in 1086.
With its neighbouring villages Stanground was very much an island
    As the sea spread across the Fens and settled on very low land.
Stanground or whatever its names and history goes back a very long way
    There was once found the remains of a Roman kiln amongst the clay.
In the 17th century there was much evidence of prehistoric implements found
    With centuries old battle-shaped axes found well underground.
Stanground created its own history when Hereward the Wake visited the place
    He couldn't have been much impressed looking at all the space.
To reach Stanground he came by boat on the river from Ely so the story goes
    What his first feelings were on seeing it no-one really knows.
The Vikings visited Stanground as a Vikings longship was found nearby
    I wonder what became of the crew or maybe they came to die.
It's known that the Romans lived in Stanground in the high ground to the east
    To celebrate on finding such a place they may have had a feast.
Through the centuries this small Saxon village has grown quite considerably
    With over 16,000 people living there now quite contentedly.
Before the county change in 1974 Stanground was then in Huntingdonshire
    Now it's part of Peterborough in the county of Cambridgeshire.

ROOTS

Stanground in Peterborough is where I was born and bred
    And the name of that village is permanently in my head.
I have countless memories that never seem to fade away
    As I continue to think of my parents in a special way.
Born at 48 Church Street is an address I'll always remember
    I being the third of four sons born to Tom and Edna.
If I was good or bad growing up is not for me to speculate
    But I know four brothers had much to celebrate.
Four such boys in Stanground who were incredibly lucky
    And to be born where we were was hardly unlucky.
Tony, Michael, Brian and Gordon were all born in that order
    Five years between each didn't cause much disorder.
Now years later my Mother and Father are long since dead
    So I have a thousand memories to be written or said.
With the passing of time my love for my parents grows
    As I think of days past with many highs and lows.
Memories privately cherished that I simply must write down
    And I sincerely hope I shall not look like a clown.
My memory still alert does hardly diminish one single day
    But sometimes it really does seem another world away.
My parents couldn't have been better if handpicked to suit
    Yes, I'm a Stanground boy and I'm proud of my roots.
I'd like to thank God for the loving start in life he gave me
    Because to be born where I was I'd won the lottery.

WHERE THE RIVER BENDS

Where the river bends is where the River Nene flows through Stanground
It stretches under a black bridge that carries a railway sound.
A new River Nene was cut in 1728 as a more direct route to Guyhirn
Cutting out the old River Nene which had many twists and turns.
Stanground has been linked to the River Nene for hundreds of years
And its prominence as a place to live often brought fears.
As south of the river was the rough side of the city I was always told
This included Stanground whose reputation could be cold.
This was disrespectful and untrue as I'd heard such stories many times
Evidently to live across the water we were a different kind.
Stanground's name years ago gave the impression of a bleak place
That's hardly fair as so much depends on people's tastes.
Thank God we were dissimilar as my birthplace had no time for snobs
We had a wonderful community spirit and very few yobs.
I'd always heard of these peculiar sayings on my growing up there
My village had developed a certain name which was unfair.
Admittedly Stanground in certain parts could be quite a rough place
Sometimes fist fights did occur but it wasn't always the case.
North Street with its three public houses could be a big attraction
And the occasional punch-up may have brought satisfaction.
Fletton and Woodston, also South of the river, never had that name
Yet I thought these areas all looked very much the same.
Years ago if one lived there one could be called a Stanground water rat
Obviously being near the river had something to do with that.
"Never visit Stanground when it rains" was always a regular saying
But being a boy there I was always well content on staying.
Stanground in the rain is not unlike other areas I would have thought
But Stanground in sunshine down by the river can't be bought.

MY FATHER (A MASTER BUTCHER)

Many years ago my Father was known as a Master butcher in his day
    And even now for some butchers that name will not go away.
His Father before him had a butchers shop in Peterborough for years
    But at that time there was much unemployment amongst the fears.
Dad arrived in Stanground in the 1920s with his wife to open a meat shop
    And times were really tough then as that business was all he'd got.
Being self-employed he was open most hours and was never one for shirking
    Simply, he wasn't a lazy man who always seemed to be working.
His butchers shop was extremely old with its thatched straw roof
    He knew his shop was in poor condition and didn't need further proof.
But as the years progressed by he built a really decent shop trade
    Enticing the public into his shop with the sausages he'd made.
Dad's customers were such a faithful lot and not prone to go elsewhere
    But sometimes we would lose one and that would make him swear.
My Father might well lecture a customer by waving his butcher's knife
    He enjoyed an argument as he frightened that person out of his life.
There were four butchers shops in Stanground which didn't please my Dad
    Four butchers selling the same could be tough when times were bad.
When Tony and Michael left school they joined Dad in the butchering
    And both would help their Father if there was any slaughtering.
Cattle were killed in his slaughterhouse and put down without delay
    Dad was too much of a human person to let cattle suffer in any way.
He always kept chickens in his yard and were killed at Christmas time
    So if a customer could afford a chicken that was a welcome sign.
If there was one thing he liked above all others it was his beloved pipe
    And between serving customers he'd nip outside to strike a light.
In the 1950s the old shop came down and replaced by a new butchers shop
    He'd worked hard for that shop so the old shop was soon forgot.
Now years later if Dad could see that shop it might reduce him to tears
    As it is now derelict and hardly recognisable from earlier years.

Dad was a well-liked and respected man and known for his butchers shop
   Which was also in Church Street with his name across the top.
Every evening my Father would venture out for his usual pint of beer
   And once inside "The Golden Lion" he moved up a gear.
With his beloved pipe in one hand and a full glass of bitter in the other
   And many times when asked was always ready for another.
He really loved the company of that pub after a hard day at the shop
   A couple of pints or maybe more but he knew when to stop.
A regular drinker I never did see my Dad drunk as he could hold his beer
   He knew when he'd had enough and departed in good cheer.
Another pub my Dad used but now closed was "The Blue Bell" in South Street
   And Mrs Slack the daughter of the landlord then, I did recently meet.
She is now ninety-seven and has a most remarkable memory for her age
   She lavished compliments about my Dad which was high praise.
Dad was a proud and good man and most conscious of the family name
   From a well-known family, he expected his sons to be the same.
He emphatically demanded respect but a strict disciplinarian - no way
   But when he put his foot down, we had to watch what to say.
He must have made a decent living though with all his boys well fed
   So they never ever went hungry when it was time for bed.
Dad was firm but fair and contented family man who loved my Mother
   She returned that love to him and never wanted another.

MY MOTHER

My Mother was a country girl who thought Peterborough was a big city
    She came from Alconbury Weston, which is known to be pretty.
When she arrived in Peterborough, an innocent girl she must have been
    And when she married my Father she felt just like a Queen.
Early in marriage their happiness complete, she gave birth to a daughter
    At her death at four it must have felt like a lamb to the slaughter.
Because of this horrid accident it shook my Mother's faith so it seemed
    And years later my parents could still hear her screams.
Eileen's tragic death must have been such a cruel and devastating blow
    So how my parents recovered from it I'll never know.
The four boys never did know her as this happened before we were born
    But over the years Mum would break down and become forlorn.
When I think of that accident I really can get distressed and annoyed
    Because to have had a big sister I'd have been overjoyed.
In a Peterborough cemetery a little angel called Eileen is laid to rest
    But years of neglect have left that cemetery in an awful mess.
Memories of my hardworking Mother continue to linger to this day
    And I'm never likely to forget that Monday was washday.
She was up at the crack of dawn on a Monday and never seemed to stop
    As my Mother kept going all day until she nearly dropped.
What with ceaseless amounts of washing, ironing and cooking all day
    She certainly never had too much time to stop for play.
My Mother would constantly scrub and toil to keep her house clean
And she really was quite a human washing machine.
She was a good and old-fashioned cook who took after her Mother
    And with her Yorkshire puddings being like no other.
So with her increasingly large family bedtime for her was often late
    And when she retired to bed she would be in a tired state.
A cousin called Kathleen then lived with us whilst working in a factory
    With her helping the war effort being most satisfactory.
During those early years of my life my Mother was often not well
    So at times to make the effort to keep going could be hell.
Mum's workload increased even more when Derek Bishop appeared
    One more mouth to feed - and he stayed for eight years.

THE EVACUEE

Derek Bishop arrived from London as a seven-year-old evacuee
    He was a big lad being nearly two years older than me.
Evacuees came to stay with Peterborough families during the blitz
    The homes some finished up at rarely resembled the Ritz.
Five thousand evacuees arrived in Peterborough in September 1939
    They would hopefully be put with families who were kind.
I can recall that day we met him at Peterborough Railway Station
    The station was full of children and I was full of elation.
The excitement I felt was that I'd be getting a brand new friend
    From London of all places so I hoped we would blend.
Imagine those evacuees leaving their homes at such a tender age
    All alone on a train they must have felt terribly strange.
In some homes evacuees were unhappy and treated in a poor way
    But Derek settled so well with us he was intending to stay.
I remember he spoke with a posh London accent when he arrived
    So he then became one of us and that's how he survived.
Together in the Church choir he had the most serene voice imaginable
    The congregation was enchanted by something so magical.
Whenever I hear the carol "Once in Royal David's City" I think of him
    With the first verse being sung by Derek who so loved to sing.

My Father's thatched butchers shop was nearly opposite our house
    The house with lots of activity was never as quiet as a mouse.
My parents insisted we all mucked in with daily chores to be done
    Derek had his share of jobs as no one escaped my Mum.
One of our jobs was cutting the lawn when it was at its thickest
    Then it was great as we could then play football or cricket.
A wonderful storyteller Derek kept Gordon and I well entertained
    Into his world of make-believe we were the ones to gain.
As the years rolled by he was never happier than in my Father's shop
    He was in his pomp as a butcher's boy and thought he'd found his lot.
My Father would agree that Derek was a big help to him during the war
    With Tony in the Forces Derek was pleased with what he saw.
With Michael and my Father he would help in making the cooked meats
    Like brawn and haslets being just two of special treats.
Then when he was fourteen and the war over his parents took him back
    And after eight years with us that seemed the end of that.
Mother thought that Derek's parents were in no hurry to take him home
    Being the longest serving evacuee locally we only had him on loan.
But I hated the idea of him leaving us and to me we were like brothers
    And I know that when he did leave us, I missed him unlike no other.
He loved butchering and leaving school that's what he should have done
    But when he returned home the encouragement he got was none.
Derek had become one of my family as he and I became really close
    And when he returned to London I missed him the most.

Looking North to Church Street from South Street on Police Station Corner

Joe Croxford's Manor House Farm in Church Street. Probably the finest stone house in Stanground

The jitty from the Lode leading into Church Street

Top end of Church Street leading up to the conker trees and the Church

STANGROUND IN WAR TIME

The outbreak of the Second World War, I was nearly five years old
    I can't remember much up to then, only what I was told.
Times would be extremely hard with my parents telling me so
    With very little money about and food rationing stocks were low.
The Government brought in ration books so no-one could overeat
    This went on throughout the war, but Mum still got us sweets.
In my Dad's butchers shop meat like other foods was in short supply
    Virtually all the food was rationed, there being not much to buy.
Petrol was scarce and only certain people could use a vehicle
    Dad had his butchers round so for him to have a van was logical.
The carrier bike was also used to deliver customers joints of meat
    With Michael and Derek sweating profusely cycling the streets.
I suppose with my Father's butchers shop his family wouldn't starve
    But even he had to be careful as the Sunday joint he carved.

The young men of Stanground in 1939 were being called up for war
    It being horrendous for some in view of what they saw.
Some didn't return and their names read out in church on Armistice Day
    What a dreadful and ultimate price those men had to pay.
Tony having joined Dad's business was called from his butcher's round
    How relieved we were when after five years he was home safe and sound.
I'd heard of the tyrant Hitler's name who was an evil man for sure
    With his funny moustache and jackboots being the cause of the war.
I can recall Churchill's name being spoken as if it were only yesterday
    As the war, the main conversation, often brought tears of dismay.
What the war did bring to Stanground was comradeship like elsewhere
    People being generally helpful and friendly everywhere.
This marvellous comradeship was a bond that held all folk together
    There being lots to talk about regardless of the weather.
Neighbours sitting on doorsteps talking well into the evening light
    This procedure was carried on every Summers night.

AIR-RAID SHELTERS

The start of the war my Father built an air-raid shelter on our lawn
    This being an inspiration of his for the oncoming storm.
Streets across Britain when the bombs fell had air-raid shelters
    In order to build such a shelter my Dad needed helpers.
His idea being that friends and neighbours could use this facility
    It was to hold twenty people and being built caused curiosity.
A hole was dug which went 8 yards into the ground and 10 yards square
    And it caused many onlookers just to stand and stare.
When it rained though water leaked through the roof causing a mess
    And the shelter seemed permanently flooded at best.
Eventually because of this excessive water the shelter caved in
    Which consequently left my Father in a bit of a spin.
Then the whole thing was abandoned and the shelter filled in again
    The lawn was re-grassed and everything looked the same.

My Father not to be beaten managed to get hold of a large steel table
    It took up half the living room and looked strong and stable.
When the air-raid siren went off informing people the enemy was above
    The family woke up and dived under the table hardly needing a shove.
Also under that table was my baby brother Gordon, a most recent arrival
    And it's quite possible my Mother would be clutching a Bible.
My parents would think what sort of world Gordon had been born into
    But thousands of parents would think the same, not just a few.
It was a dark, threatening world and no one could see what was imminent
    Prayers said in air-raid shelters would often act as a stimulant.
My Father's idea of a steel table was in case our house was hit by a bomb
    We had some protection but a direct hit, we would all be gone.
We might stay under the table until the air-raid siren gave the all clear
    And then as one we might sigh with relief and offer a cheer.

GAS MASKS

When war was declared with Germany free gas masks were supplied
   Everyone had a gas mask in the hope they would survive.
Civilians were encouraged to carry their gas masks everywhere
   If the enemy dropped poisonous gasses we had to beware.
This necessary procedure was carried out throughout Great Britain
   And if gas bombs were dropped the country would be smitten.
With the carrying of gas masks people would be ready for an attack
   They were made of rubber and usually the colour of black.
Although not compulsory people were to carry them on their person
   But they were so uncomfortable and looked terribly irksome.
Today those gas masks would look like something from out of space
   The mask had big goggled eyes with a tube hanging down the face.
Even at school all children were being taught how to use the masks
   Then the masks were tried and tested in a chamber of gas.
A big mobile van was parked outside the school so we all went inside
   Quite an experience it was to think the gas really was live.
One problem being was how to get babies to wear those gas masks
   It really was quite inhuman to try and ask of such a task.
Gas attacks were expected from the enemy at the start of the war
   But fortunately they were never put to the test for sure.
Germany never resorted to such gas attacks like the First World War
   But those gas masks were horrible to wear and were sore.
Surely though Britain had to be prepared for any eventuality
   So those gas masks were much more than a formality.

GERMAN BOMBERS

German aircraft I can clearly remember on really cold winter nights
    They seemed above our house which always gave me a fright.
Minutes after the air-raid siren went we could hear them in the distance
    And Britain at this time couldn't offer too much resistance.
Those German bomber planes had a deep humming monotonous sound
    Which grew louder over Stanground being Midlands bound.
Every night for a while they flew over Peterborough to bomb Coventry
    And on bombing that city to near oblivion is now history.
If they had wanted they could have bombed Peterborough into submission
    But they were after bigger fish, that was their obvious mission.
On hearing bomber planes above my Father would be quite forthright
    And he'd say "Coventry are going to get it again tonight".
Returning to Germany a plane dropped a bomb over Stanground later
    Half the village came out next day to see that bomb crater.
The crater was a massive hole as many people gathered round to see
    It landed in Mount Pleasant missing the church and terrified me.
What I can recall is the strange silence of everyone looking at the hole
    No-one uttered a word which was really an ugly looking bowl.
The bomb landed a few hundred yards from our house taught us a lesson
    And looking at the crater left a deep and lasting impression.
Fortunately by a stroke of good luck no one was killed or even maimed
    But the war had come to Stanground and things wouldn't be the same.
To sit in an air-raid shelter with bombers above felt threatening
    And just to hear those aircraft could be frightening.

WINSTON CHURCHILL

Stanground in war time were my very first reflections of life
    With Hitler's bomber planes continuing to bring strife.
Not that I can recall any more bombs being dropped near us
    But in cities these bombs were creating more than a fuss.
Big cities like London were being bombed on a regular basis
    Many killed as people scanned the newspapers for the latest.
My early Stanground years were really of such a happy place
    As everyone who lived there would agree that was the case.
Comradeship was everything as people helped as never before
    But everyone was naturally concerned about the war.
Neighbours were there for each other if there was anything to be done
    Where today the friendliness of some neighbours is often none.
It didn't matter too much if someone forgot to lock the back door
    Because nothing was ever stolen – and of that I'm sure.
In those so frightful times life proceeded on with optimism and hope
    As we gathered around the wireless when Winston Churchill spoke.
He was Britain's Prime Minister during the many gloomy war years
    What an inspirational figure to lift the nation above the tears.
Churchill I felt was at his best with his dynamic wartime speeches
    Who can forget when he said " we will fight them on the beaches".
And his memorable "We will never surrender" the great man said
    How very fortunate we were to have him as our head.
My Father during those dark days was a committed Churchillian
    He always said "cometh the hour, cometh the man".
At England's despairing time of need we had Churchill I was told
    Because of him British people needed to be cheerful and bold.
I very much doubt whether Churchill had ever heard of Stanground
    We knew of him all right and his voice was an uplifting sound.
Would we have defeated Germany without Churchill I'm not sure
    But his bulldog spirit was more than Hitler bargained for.
And surely one doesn't necessarily have to be too elementary
    To hail him as one of the greatest men of the last century.

THE SPECIALS

Known as "The Specials" they were attached to the local Police Force
    As they patrolled a certain area which was part of their course.
They were all volunteers and patrolled the streets in evening time
    So with everywhere in darkness and lights out it could be a bad sign.
Sometimes German bombers were about and air raid sirens would blow
    People quickly vanished off the streets as that noise told them so
So Police Specials were primarily required to patrol the streets
    My Father then joined The Specials and other Specials he'd meet.
He wanted to help with the war effort but the Home Guard he didn't join
    As volunteers were wanted when the Police Specials were formed.
I think being a Special it appeared to him that he could help locally
    And he took his position most seriously and committed totally.
Although he had his butchers shop it meant he became a Special part time
    I can just about remember him in his police uniform looking so fine.
On discarding his butchers apron he'd report to the Police Station
    To be paired off with another Special and then find their location.
His patch being a part of Stanground but also some of Fletton too
    Then challenged anyone out on the streets during a long curfew.
On walking the streets with another Special they were often tested
    As anyone whom they saw being suspicious could be arrested.
I think my Father quite enjoyed doing his bit and keen to help the war
    He had fought in the First World War and never forgot what he saw.
If I can remember correctly he'd be out about four evenings a week
    Occasionally he might be out all night and then have little sleep.
But these Specials to my knowledge were spread throughout the land
    And patrolling their areas on foot their patch was well manned.

POVERTY

Looking back over sixty years my memory is generally still good
    Being spared Alzheimer's means my brain to be as it should.
Etched on my mind are my early days and the extreme poverty
    Kids with holes in their clothes was hardly equality.
Some had holes in their trousers with half their bottoms showing
    It could be terribly embarrassing for kids still growing.
Large holes also appeared in their socks and in their shoes too
    And in the Winter the children looked so full of flu.
Mums everywhere were forever sewing with patching to be done
    If only to try to cover up their children's thin little bum.
In some homes there might not even be enough food on the table
    Definitely not enough to keep kids strong and able.
With food being rationed it meant that times were so often grim
    It was wartime in Britain and all kids became thin.
Larger families suffered the most and became dreadfully poor
    Some men were not even working and many in the war.
There was certainly no overweight children like there is today
    And undernourished families desperately needed more pay.
This hardship spread throughout Britain with all being affected
    Until the war was won, this could not be corrected.
And many families might well have been overcrowded in one bed
    With no central heating kids cuddled up to keep warm instead.
A regular sight was to see Stanground women collect coal in a pram
    Admittedly it was an old pram, but they had no man.
On pushing it to a Fletton Coal Yard they would load it with coal
    But Winters were harsh, so that walk was hardly a stroll.
Thinking about those days it all now seems another world to me
    There being such anguish amongst so much poverty.
But above all the poverty there was this marvellous comradeship
    As Stanground people did much more than their little bit.
Strange when I say I am very pleased I was born in such times
    Because I now value what I've got and that is not a crime.
Believe me some families in Stanground were so near destitution
    Not like a third world country but there was desperation.

JAM JARS

As the war progressed further there was much despair, grief and misery
    With families making endless sacrifices usually most cheerfully.
Families had to cut back on many things with our home not excluded
    So if one thought there might be a Christmas present, one was deluded.
Now during the war many things were obsolete or scarce of that I know
    As our home was dominated by males the best tea set was never on show.
This was because Mum's other tea sets and china cups had all been broken
    Her clumsy boys had broken them washing up, so harsh words were spoken.
Mum lost so much crockery with all those cups and saucers being dropped
    That she was prepared to try alternatives for this farce to stop.
The sacrifice she made was that for cups of tea, old jam jars were to be used
    So we always had our tea in jam jars and at first we were bemused.
Other families because of the shortage of cups would try something similar
    But by the end of the war we got so used to those jars as they were familiar.
I might add that if we had visitors the best tea set regularly came out
    With the visitors gone the tea set disappeared with no messing about.
When the war was over crockery and china cups were again seen in the shops
    So the drinking of tea in those jam jars then proceeded to stop.
Those old jam jars never broke when they accidentally slipped out of one's hand
    But I admit to get back to cups and saucers again it was grand.
These little incidents as I write continue still to come flooding back
    But with tea in jam jars I'd conveniently forgotten all that.

THE YANKS ARE HERE

They would cruise around Stanground in their big American cars
    Yes the G.I.s had arrived and they made for the bars.
I can well remember their cars going up and down Church Street
    The Yanks were interested in the girls they could meet.
One couldn't fail to notice them as I began to see more of G.I. Joe
    They were resented at first because they seemed all show.
They were forever chewing gum and called everyone Bud or Mac
    The British being more reserved had little time for that.
Being stationed locally they quickly became quite a familiar sight
    As thousands seemed to arrive in Britain overnight.
In 1942 they arrived after the Japanese attack on Pearl Harbour
    America being drawn into the war before it progressed further.
With their smart uniforms the Yanks were popular with the girls
    So with their reputation they tried to give more than pearls.
These American G.I.s always seemed to have plenty of money
    As many British girls were often addressed as honey.
They had more money than our troops which added to their glamour
    Good looking and brash I never did hear one stammer.
I've heard it said about the Yanks, over here, over paid and over-sexed
    So searching for English girls was for them a major quest.
British troops couldn't compete of course with the G.I.s lifestyles
    Some people failed to understand them by many a mile.
There was some real indignation against them in the early days
    Seemingly flash the locals rightly resented their ways.
One big problem was that British men were away fighting the war
    As the Yanks began chasing Peterborough girls even more.
"Got any gum chum" became a favourite phrase of all kids locally
    And the G.I.s always so generous responded totally.

G.I. BRIDES

G.I.s were stationed at Connington, Polebrook and Molesworth
    It meant local girls leaving the country of their birth.
Many Peterborough girls went to America to become G.I. brides
    I've often wondered what became of their lives.
I can remember some Stanground girls quite clearly even now
    Lovely girls too as they took their marriage vows.
Some of those brides would be only 17 or 18 years of age
    To be whisked off to America were heady days.
They didn't leave Britain until 1945 which was after the war
    I wonder if they were prepared for what they saw.
There were stories some were unhappy with what they found there
    Yet others took to the U.S. at their very first stare.
I think the glamour of being a G.I.s wife was soon phased out
    As some G.I.s promised a future they could dream about.
Once there they found some G.I.s came from the humblest of homes
    Some found poverty which only added to their woes.
British girls went to America full of excitement as G.I. brides
    One thing is sure it improved British-American ties.
Yet after the war when the Yanks returned home there was sadness
    Friendships formed with local families brought much gladness.
With the war over there developed a bond with the two countries
    Forged in the defeat of Germany had stirred consciences.
The special relationship between Britain and America exists today
    Those Young G.I. brides had more than paved the way.

AMERICAN ICON

It's not always known that at Polebrook a great movie icon was stationed
  He flew many missions over Germany and wasn't on a vacation.
In 1939 his latest and greatest film "Gone with the Wind" was released
  And the rave notices for playing Rhett Butler never ceased.
The undisputed King of Hollywood, his film was hailed the greatest ever
  With box office takings proving the film will last forever.
At the height of his film career he must have felt reasonably satisfied
  And what he did next his actions were certainly justified.
Not for him brooding at home having lost his career because of the war
  So the American public were pleased with what they saw.
It wasn't long after that film he then signed up for the American Air Force
  And Major Clark Gable was determined to complete the course.
Stationed at Polebrook and seen in Peterborough, ladies' hearts would flutter
  Evidently women on seeing him their legs would melt like butter.
I'm sure he didn't spend his time in England in his car cruising around
  If he did I wonder if he found a Scarlett O'Hara in Stanground.

Hollywood heartthrob

STREET PARTIES

The war in Europe officially ended on the 8th May 1945
    I would have known little else being born in 1935.
Britain celebrated with street parties for children everywhere
    Church Street being no exception had its fair share.
Memory tells me that the party in our street was near V.E. day
    As about forty children started eating without delay.
Although food was rationed the makeshift tables had a good spread
    Mothers helping out made more than just bread.
With sandwiches and fancy cakes we were being spoilt to death
    As whatever was put on the table nothing was left.
The tables and chairs were situated halfway along Church Street
    With Hitler defeated it was more than just a treat.
Entertainment was laid on with countless games and races to be won
    The excitement so evident as all joined in the fun.
No more air-raid sirens or shelters to disturb everyone's sleep
    As the country went ecstatic but others had a weep.
Husbands and sons in Stanground never did return from the war
    They paid the ultimate price as casualties became more.
With Derek, Gordon and myself the party was a special occasion
    As kids everywhere felt much elated with this jubilation.
On that day there were thanksgiving services throughout the land
    Some street parties were even supported by a band.
Although the war with Germany was over it dragged on in the Far East
    Then America dropped an atomic bomb so hostilities ceased.
So for Stanground being like elsewhere the war was finally over
    As the country got back to normal with everyone more sober.

THE PARISH CHURCH

Driving my car South along the Parkway, my eyes focus on a church
    It's always second nature to look left as I never have to search.
It stands in all its glory the very impressive Stanground Church steeple
    So proud it stands above the trees a place of worship for the people.
This 14th century Parish Church of St John the Baptist is serenely beautiful
    By far the oldest building in Stanground and its more than suitable.
Just to stand and admire this grandest of churches is a work of art
    How did they build such buildings years ago and to make them last.
Built of Barnack stone I'm sure the Church will stand hundreds of years
    These old Churches will stand the test of time with hardly any fears.
Stanground Church bells were always regarded as the finest in the area
    And to hear other church bells chime seemed less superior.
I have a certain affection for that Church that goes back a long way
    As my Mum insisted on a Sunday I attend Church three times a day.
Being in the Church choir for seven years I felt on some sort of mission
    My Brothers and Derek had spells in the choir so it was a tradition.
Mum being a keen church lady meant she took her religion seriously
    So when Sunday arrived she attended church most cheerfully.
Her attitude with her sons attending Church we would make good Christians
    If this is the case then hopefully we have turned out decent citizens.
Being so very young to sit through three church services could be boring
    And with other boys in the choir we couldn't stop yawning.
When I was really little playing in the churchyard was always good fun
    But if the vicar, Morley Wells, appeared we did a quick run.
Hiding behind gravestones in the churchyard I can remember the most
    I was somewhat nervous though that I might see a ghost.
In the week now the church is locked up and not to keep out the odd rat
    Unfortunately vandalism being the main instigator for that.

The Stanground Parish Church in Church Street

A service is being held inside the St. John's the Baptist Church. The author attended services three times a day as a choir boy on Sundays and felt he knew every inch of this beautiful church

The old Vicarage in Church Street now a Polish Club

North Street looking west with 'The Woolpack' on the right

Two of the magnificent seven that was

North Street facing east, the white building on the left is 'The Ferryboat', now demolished along with many houses either side of the street

'The Anchor Inn' in North Street, now a private house

A man with his boats, the legendary Vic Jackson of North Street was a well-known boat builder,along the banks of the river Nene, where boats called regularly at his boatyard for repairs;

These thatched cottages in Mount Pleasant have long been demolished, still standing is Jack Goodwins Nursery House

Chapel Street school where the author has fond memories of sixty years ago

The Baptist Church on the corner of Chapel Street and Church Street

MORLEY WELLS

One of the great characters of Stanground was Morley Wells
    This reverent vicar had been known to ring the church bells.
He would stride around the village as if he owned the place
    Speaking to everyone who had much time and space.
With his walking stick he would walk Stanground raising his hat
    With his dog trailing behind him whose name was Mac.
A dedicated priest who really tried to increase his congregation
    But the response he received was hardly a celebration.
He first came to England from Canada during the First World War
    And in the Army was badly wounded from what he saw.
Returning after the war he settled in England and became a priest
    So he came to Stanground as his Army career had ceased.
Whenever he saw my Father he raised his hat, pleasing my Dad
    Dad also in that war thought how much in common they had.
I know my Father respected the vicar for having been in the war
    So my Dad in conversation never found him such a bore.
The vicar had a big booming voice which was heard on many a day
    As his voice could be heard several times down your way.
Morley Wells was undoubtedly a true character from my early life
    Being in the church choir I can clearly remember his wife.
His wife's name was Queenie whose name before marriage was Cavell
    Edith, a cousin, was shot by the Germans in her captivity in hell.
So there stands in Peterborough the so very fine Edith Cavell Hospital
    In memory of a brave nurse who found the enemy inhospitable.
For me therefore Morley Wells and Edith Cavell are linked together
    Just two names which I'm sure I'll remember forever.

THE BLACK BRIDGE

The Black Bridge in Stanground was quite a landmark years ago
 And if anyone enjoyed swimming it was the place to go.
To be swimming in the River Nene was undoubtedly a special treat
 If only to get away from other sports I played on the street.
The bridge over the river carried L.N.E.R. and L.M.S. railway trains
 Though swimming under the bridge the noise could be a pain.
People would change into their swimming gear on the river bank
 Sometimes though the river wasn't clean and often stank.
I learned to swim under that bridge and spent many hours there
 And to dive off the very top one had beaten any scare.
In Summer it really was a popular place and the hotter the better
 And those hot steamy days one didn't need a sweater.
Sunday afternoons was best because it was picnics on the river bank
 Watching the occasional boat go cruising by and it never sank.
Youngsters and adults of all ages often played and swam together
 Everyone feeling perfectly safe and enjoying the weather.
There was never a fear that a child could be harmed in any way
 And the name of paedophile was simply a world away.
I remember playing in the fields near the bridge until it was dark
 Our parents never worried we would do anything for a lark.
Many people would sit on the riverbank as I have memories galore
 The dark days had disappeared as we recovered from the war.
The old Black Bridge burnt down for more years than I remember
 But those old memories I'll never surrender.

ENTERTAINMENT

So what did Stanground people do for entertainment after the war
    Money so scarce some didn't venture any further than the front door.
The radio, then a wireless, played a significant part in our lives
    It was very much the only entertainment for housebound wives.
There was Dick Barton Special Agent on for five evenings a week
    Kids found that $1/4$ hour so exciting that afterwards couldn't sleep.
I.T.M.A. with the Liverpool comedian Tommy Handley was a popular show
    The comedians then were really funny, not like today's all-time low.
With no TV and other luxuries the wireless would be on in many homes
    And let's not forget that very few homes would have a telephone.
An evening out at the pictures brought much pleasure in those days
    One night a week with long queues for the flicks my memory says.
There were three cinemas in town and in Woodston there was the Savoy
    As courting couples snogged in the back double seats in untold joy.
Whist drives, card games and dominoes were played in people's houses
    A few coins might have been played for causing a few grouses.
The Parish Room in Church Street was used for many social activities
    Which would have included over the years many festivities.
There were seven pubs in Stanground which might put on entertainment
    With probably a pianist on the piano singing for his payment.
Weekends people might go to town to the river embankment for a walk
    The embankment drew crowds of people who indulged in much talk.
Wicksteed Park for a day with its amusements was not to be missed
    A lovely time was had by all there with picnics in such bliss.
Going to Hunstanton or Skegness was always a very special day out
    Certainly not a Costa del Sol but most had a good time no doubt.
To travel to these seaside resorts I remember was quite magical
    To get that first look of the sea kids would go near hysterical.
And to walk on the seafront at Hunstanton it was very obvious to see
    With many local people there it felt like Peterborough-on-Sea.

FAILURE AT SCHOOL

At school it quickly became apparent I hadn't got an academic mind
  I was beginning to think nature might have been unkind.
But nature has been good to me as I was born with all my faculties
  With the constant energy I had I was hardly born a casualty.
I therefore attended two schools in Stanground when I was a boy
  Neither of these schools filled me with any ultimate joy.
So it didn't take long to come to the conclusion I wasn't very bright
  To have seen any of my schoolwork was not a pretty sight.
I started at the infant school which was nearly opposite the church
  Lucky for me it was that the school never had the birch.
At the senior school in Chapel Street my schoolwork was abysmal
  Any school report I may have had continued to be dismal.
Mathematics was particularly difficult as my brain didn't function
  So because of that I rarely seemed to have any gumption.
History, geography and English I really was a complete and utter flop
  When is all this silly nonsense I thought going to stop.
Quite early in my school days I decided I must be as thick as a plank
  Always in the bottom three so I certainly couldn't swank.
I'm ashamed to say that every subject at school was difficult for me
  I was no scholar but a cricketer or footballer I wanted to be.
What were my parents to do with me as I nose-dived from bad to worse
  Being rather a hopeless case they had every right to curse.
By my attitude my parents must have been hurt and so disappointed
  My enjoyment was sports as my classwork left me haunted.
On taking the eleven-plus my parents didn't really expect me to pass
  Sure enough I didn't and should have been kicked up the ****.
I then lost confidence and felt a shocking failure at this time of strife
  This failure was to stay with me throughout my early life.

IN MY DREAMS

Sport always came naturally to me as I adapted to any sport going
    Cricket and soccer an absolute must while still growing.
I'm not saying I was any good at sports as I've never had need to boast
    So on reflection I think I was just about ordinary at most.
From school on hot afternoons I'd run home to get my cricket bat
    And with pals ran about all evening hoping I wouldn't get fat.
We would play near the conker trees with the church wall for wickets
    Then we would run in and bowl to prove who was quickest.
There was also a big field at the rear of my Father's butchers shop
    And we would play until it was dark or until we dropped.
I think of Peter Fairchild who was about my age in Church Street
    As we always seemed to play cricket whenever we did meet.
In that field we would fantasize about our heroes for many hours
    The only thing to bother us would be the odd few showers.
In that field I'd play sport with Ray Woods when we were just children
    We never thought that years later we'd share three grandchildren.
My enthusiasm for cricket meant I couldn't get enough of the game
    That's how it's been all my life as my love never wanes.
At Chapel Street School I eventually got into the cricket team
    Being a lousy scholar, I had to shine at something to be seen.
A schoolteacher called Tom Nutt coached us how to play the game
    He gave his valuable time to us and treated us all the same.
We once played on the famed Peterborough Town Cricket Club ground
    And we had John Craythorne whose batting was so sound.
To play cricket on that lovely old ground was so exciting, I swear
    Years later I'd joined that club and spent many years there.
Tony Moulds who became a good local cricketer bowled sides out
    Tony died a few years ago and he's still missed terribly no doubt.
With my great love of cricket my classwork deteriorated even more
    In my dreams I wondered how many runs would Len Hutton score.
He was my hero and England's best, if only I could bat like him I thought
    What a disappointment when I kept getting out for nought.

MY CHURCH STREET

Some mornings John Collins would herd his cattle down our street
    He was a farmer and no one could describe his cows sweet.
This happened twice a day as he regularly brought them back again
    Having messed up the street once, cows have no shame.
The stinking cow dung in Church Street was scattered all over the place
    With everywhere such a mess as cows only walk one pace.
Like being on the fairground dodgems as one tried to dodge the muck
    If one fell over one invariably got more than just stuck.
This odious mess would make the most foul smell imaginable
    And with cats and dogs about anything was possible.
I'm equally sure though that most homes had a cat or a dog in those days
    Many roaming the street being nothing more than strays.
So there were plenty of smells about as it didn't pay to breathe easily
    Otherwise there could be the possibility of feeling queasy.
Rats always a menace might also appear in Church Street years ago
    And to see a chicken crossing the street added to the glow.
A man called Churchie would then pull his veg cart up our street
    Shouting out loud selling vegetables and watching his feet.
With few motor vehicles these were the days of the horse and cart
    Trudging up Church Street one might well blow a …...
Because of John Collins'cattle Church Street at times was dirty
    People living there could then become quite shirty.
Several horses during the day would do its excrement on our street
    Horses never shy on manure made the scene complete.

ON THE STREET WHERE I LIVED

The five shops in Church Street would sell anything from bread to sweets
　　To have any money as children and use those shops was a real treat.
How on earth those five corner general shops scraped a living I don't know
　　For shopkeepers when trade was bad would reach an all-time low.
Church Street had the Post Office in Stanground so there was often a queue
　　Sometimes the Post Office could be loaded with people and not just a few.
There were two butchers shops in Church Street with one being my Dad's
　　Opposite his shop was a bakery so the smell from baked bread wasn't bad.
Queues would congregate outside Freemans Fish Shop to buy fish and chips
　　The fish tasted so good that it must have come straight off a fishing ship.
Fish and chips must have been a real cheap meal during and after the war
　　As wherever there was a fish and chip shop there were queues I'm sure.
The local Bobby lived in Church Street so did a School Teacher and the Vicar
　　Also there was a Haulage Contractor, a Postman, a Plumber and a Fitter.
Years after the war Jack Warrington opened a shop and he was a TV Engineer
　　He was one of the first to sell TVs and he should have been a millionaire.
I can well recall a woman who lived near us who had been recently divorced
　　Divorce was something shameful then and not necessarily her choice.
Looking out from the rear of our house was a beautifully kept garden nursery
　　Owned by the Goodwins and it housed many sizeable conservatories.
Opposite our house was an elderly gentleman who had been a Cabinet Maker
　　And in the street there was more than one family with the surname Baker.
Maybe it's my imagination but there seemed many Bakers then in Stanground
　　Probably not so many these days but I know they are still around.
The men folk had a variety of different jobs and one worked the fairgrounds
　　With Bill Barber the Builder driving his big car with its purring sound.
The same Bill Barber was always dressed in black being the local Undertaker
　　In front of the hearse he would walk which may have carried a Baker.

STANGROUND FEAST

The Stanground Feast was a major attraction once upon a time
    To gain admission in days past would cost less than a dime.
It was held to mark the dedication of the Parish Church of St John
    The original procedure of celebration has now but all gone.
It was a happy Stanground occasion with large crowds in attendance
    People supported the feast just like the Service of Remembrance.
The celebrations started with a service in the Church on a Sunday
    And carried on with events on the vicarage lawns on the Monday.
A weekend was picked out right at the height of the Summer in June
    There being excitement everywhere with no doom or gloom.
The feast was usually a success providing of course the sun came out
    And it was here that I participated in my first boxing bout.
The local school put on the boxing which was part of the entertainment
    With youngsters showing skills in the ring proving no ailment.
The feast was held in the vicarage gardens in a perfect English setting
    It always went off without a hitch with no one ever regretting.
Also supplied by the school children was much singing and dancing
    An appreciative audience responding with clapping and stamping.
There were sideshows and stalls scattered all around the lawns
    My Mother often a helper serving tea, cakes and popcorns.
The main event of the evening was probably the skittling for a pig
    Given by a local farmer as the muscle men tried to look big.
And huge wooded balls were then hurled to knock the skittles down
    Sweating profusely and failing miserably the men would frown.
This went on until 10 pm or when the pig was eventually won
    One local man having won the pig would beg or borrow a gun.
Profits from the feast helped greatly towards the costs of the Church
    So without it the Church would really be in the lurch.
It appears before I was born the feast was even bigger than in my time
    With brass bands walking up Church Street in a processional line.
With vast crowds evidently turning up to watch the parade go by
    Flags flying, trumpets blowing, it must have looked good on the eye.
To finish the evening off there was a dance on the vicarage lawn
    With the end of the event finishing well before dawn.

THE GOLDEN LION

The Golden Lion pub is situated at the South end of Church Street
    And there it stands today making the scene complete.
Many of the real characters of Stanground would meet in this pub
    My Dad the local butcher knew many as it seemed he should.
The Golden Lion was built in 1935, the year incidentally I was born
    I'm sure Dad would wet the baby's head rather than cut the lawn.
Years ago I would know of these characters, but now not so clearly
    Maybe it is Alzheimer's but I'm not giving in to that theory.
What I can recall about that pub is the numbers who would use the place
    While opposite was Freemans Fish Shop who sold the real plaice.
Never being allowed into a pub it often intrigued me what went on there
    Because when it was closing the regulars were worse for wear.
"The Golden Lion" did a roaring trade with laughter and singing heard
    I'm not sure that when the money ran out if more beer was served.
Now this period just after the war for some there seemed money about
    The men might keep their wives short, so when drunk would shout.
The odd American car would then draw up and out stepped G.I. Joe
    These yanks being the centre of attention with their latest girls in tow.
In those days in Stanground some women would call at this pub with a jug
    The jug when full of beer they would get home as fast as they could.
A Mrs West and Mrs Steels every evening would call for their jug of beer
    How those old dears managed to climb up Chapel Street is not clear.
Dad would meet Sid Ellwood, a fellow butcher from Church Street there
    Although they were in competition they were friendly as a pair.
Dick Rimes, another friend of my Father was the landlord of this pub
    If people misbehaved he would call them more than just love.
I used to think to my young self what was the attraction with this beer
    Because Dad on arriving home would call my Mother dear.

THE BADGER

When a stray badger was killed on our lawn many years ago
  It may have come from the river but nobody seemed to know.
One morning I discovered on our lawn many freshly dug holes
  The holes about two foot wide were not made by moles.
I looked down one hole and saw the hairy back of an animal
  Being nine years old I didn't want to appear too affable.
I quickly called my Father and he straightaway called the Police
  A marksman then promptly arrived and shot the beast.
Some badgers had been known to attack people I was told
  It had to be put down and the thought left me cold.
Arriving home from school later a crowd was outside our house
  The badger created an interest far more than shooting grouse.
The Police had hung it up by its hind legs from the apple tree
  Many observers were on the lawn full of curiosity.
It had a most beautiful striped coat and was three and a half foot long
  On seeing it I was curious but pleased when it had gone.
I thought at my young age how sad it was to see a badger dead
  Perhaps I was too sentimental or just silly in the head.
My parents then had a rug made from the badger's lovely coat
  It laid in our house for years a reminder that I mustn't gloat.
Looking back on the animal's death I can feel quite uncomfortable
  With being the one who saw it first makes me feel responsible.

THE PARISH ROOM

Mention to me of the Parish Room and it brings back endless memories
 With wedding receptions, dances and parties being specialities.
The Parish Room in Church Street was there for all but there was a fee
 And I know the Village Cricket Team regularly used it for tea.
I can well remember many children's parties there at Christmas time
 It was such a cosy little place with the atmosphere so divine.
If my memory serves me right it was heated by a large open wood fire
 With children gathered around it until it was time for goodbye.
The Parish Room has been in existence since it was built in 1846 to date
 Once a school I'm not sure if it is used at all now, but open to debate.
The first television show I ever saw was in a very crowded Parish Room
 It really was a big attraction as television would become a boom.
I sat spell bound because it so reminded me of being at the pictures
 No one knew then that television would become a regular fixture.
The screen unfortunately was not brilliant as it was snowy at times
 But that enthusiastic audience on that day didn't seem to mind.
There could have been a hundred people or so it seemed in that room
 All crowded in for two major occasions and to lift any gloom.
So the very first TV I saw was the coronation of Queen Elizabeth II
 Everyone was straining at the neck and hardly missing a second.
Television was really in its infancy as people hadn't seen it before
 I'm not sure if one paid to get in but there was a queue at the door.
The second television programme was the F.A. Cup Final of that year
 The room was overflowing with people and generally in good cheer.
Blackpool v. Bolton was the match as all kids wanted Blackpool to win
 But it soon became apparent that Bolton's chances were very slim.
It was known as the Stanley Matthew's Final as he dazzled on the wing
 The Parish Room was in uproar with Matthews the undisputed king.

RAIDERS FROM FLETTON

Sometimes I can look back on my early life with some amazement
    And the battle in Church Lane was of some engagement.
Yes incredibly it did take place and I'd be about ten years old
    My brother Michael told me to stay clear and do as I was told.
Michael was always involved in any trouble going when he was young
    So the throwing of stones for him was just a bit of fun.
The rivalry between Stanground and Fletton boys could be intense
    When we played them at school soccer the tension was immense.
But feelings ran high, there being no love whenever the two sides met
    And throwing stones at each other was never done for a bet.
The rival gangs met either side of The Lode which is of course a dyke
    Two hundred yards apart the gangs were spoiling for a fight.
Then the throwing of small stones would begin with some bombardment
    Some would throw better than others amongst much encouragement.
How some person was never hurt or seriously wounded I'll never know
    As missiles came hurtling from the sky to strike a hard blow.
There would be dozens of boys under fourteen either side of The Lode
    This carried on for quite a few minutes then it was time to reload.
Michael told me later that this incidence was a regular occurrence
    So to stand in the line of fire was a feat of some endurance.
I might have thrown the odd stone myself but I was scared of being hit
    As those Fletton boys could well throw more than just a bit.
If that event happened now people would say what are things coming to
    I'm sure though on arriving home my first call would be the loo.

STANGROUND REC

The Stanground recreation ground was situated in Chapel Street
    Opposite the school it was where school kids would meet.
For many children coming to school from the area of North Street
    It was a short cut through the rec saving their feet.
After lunch it was a natural thing to go to the rec to play sports
    Cricket in Summer, soccer in Winter or any other sort.
During the lunch break and other times I spent many hours there
    I can still visualize dozens of kids playing without a care.
Being so bored in the classroom I would try anything to be outside
    The rec being the ideal place to escape the tediousness inside.
I can just about remember when the rec had swings and roundabouts
    To see children making their own pleasure was never in doubt.
There was no television or computer games then to keep kids amused
    So with the push button era of today we would be confused.
I look at some of the really overweight children in our schools today
    My constant fear is that obesity is sorrowfully here to stay.
And in some schools now there is hardly any physical exercise at all
    Yet when my generation was young we would be kicking a ball.
The Stanground recreation ground was a godsend for local boys
    The pleasurable time spent there gave us unlimited joy.
Extremely popular in the rec was November the 5th for bonfire night
    With rubbish and wood stacked up high waiting for a light.
There would be crowds gathered round the bonfire with fireworks galore
    And when let off into the dark sky, they would then soar.
I can also recall the annual fairground at the recreation ground
    Kids enjoying themselves in that environmental sound.
Today the Stanground rec is no more and is now a housing estate
    On visiting Chapel Street recently it was time to meditate.

THE LOCAL BOBBY

Stanground used to have a police station until it closed in 1960
    The building is now an office and it must have quite a history.
It stood on Police Station Corner and was situated in South Street
    With a policeman directing the traffic being part of his beat.
There was a jail inside the station which held some prisoners there
    To see a prisoner handcuffed people would stand and stare.
So where have the bobbies gone who patrolled our streets years ago?
    Because they certainly kept the local criminals in tow.
I personally think it's a shame that bobbies were taken off their beat
    He had his nose to the ground and could be more than discreet.
These policemen built up a reputation looking after their territory
    They would walk or cycle whatever was their priority.
The local bobby would be so familiar that many would know him
    The chances of not knowing him would be very slim.
Our local bobby was only a few hundred yards from where I lived
    And if I actually saw him I could run as fast as any kid.
He really was respected and very much part of the local community
    And I never did see him show off his superiority.
The effect he had meant our village was relatively free of any crime
    Anything reported to him would be dealt with on time.
There must have been several Stanground bobbies over the years
    And with his status in the community so high, we had no fears.

TROUBLE WITH THE LAW

To illustrate the respect the people had for their local bobby
　　Ours had once caught me smoking and I'd be sorry.
Because when my brother Tony returned from India after the war
　　I was amazed and somewhat excited with what I saw.
He'd brought a thousand cigarettes to be smoked at his leisure
　　He didn't realize that Brian would indulge in this pleasure.
I was eleven years old and to be grown up it was time to smoke
　　Even though I was years away from being able to vote.
One evening with pals we started smoking in front of my home
　　Guess who's still plodding his beat as we start to groan.
My memory is really tested as I look back over so many years
　　And what the local bobby says nearly reduces me to tears.
The copper looks at me with suspicion as if I'd stolen some loot
　　His presence makes me nervous as I shake in my boots.
"You are young Holdich aren't you" he inquisitively said to me
　　Looking guilty and stamping my fag out I had to agree.
"Let's see your Father I'm sure he doesn't know you smoke" he said
　　I sheepishly followed him probably wishing I were dead.
Now my Dad listened to this copper and immediately sent me upstairs
　　I nervously went to my bedroom and felt like saying my prayers.
What my Father said to me and instil discipline I'm not quite sure
　　I do know that no-one ever caught me smoking any more.
I suppose my early brush with the law was so very timid really
　　But that local bobby had handled it so supremely.
One can imagine a bobby reporting that incident to parents today
　　He would get abuse and told to put the real criminals away.

THE BOAT YARDS

Stanground's River Nene has always run parallel with North Street
    And with the boat yards there it makes the scene complete.
This being a busy part of Stanground which didn't lack activity
    As boats have always been repaired to the highest quality.
Before I was born the riverside catered for many boat yards there
    With boats and barges calling in for repairs to wear and tear.
The roads to Stanground in centuries past would be just tracks
    So the river was used to more than compensate that.
Boats and barges would arrive by the river for moorings there
    As grain, peat and flour was distributed with care.
The river would be used frequently to carry numerous items
    With coal, wood and stones being regular sightings.
As a boy I remember the boat yards called Lee's and Jackson's
    And at these two yards there was always plenty of action.
Once I had a glimpse of Lee's workshop and saw a boat being built
    A massive boat it was as it seemed to be on some stilts.
Vic Jackson was undoubtedly one of the characters in those days
    Working on the boats and reminiscing about his younger ways.
The boat yards are not nearly as busy as they once were in the street
    When boats and barges on the river looked more like a fleet.
Boat builders have worked in Stanground for hundreds of years
    And like all good seafaring men could sink a few beers.
These people having worked up a thirst would then drink some ale
    So the more they drank the more they told a good tale.
In the "Woolpack", "Ferryboat" and "Anchor" many a yarn was told
    The stories were so good that no one left feeling cold.
I'm pleased to write that boat yards still operate in North Street
    Without the boat yards that street would be incomplete.

NORTH STREET PEOPLE

Many of Stanground's residents lived in houseboats on the River Nene
　　With so many houseboats moored along the river bank to be seen.
Houseboats were to be lived in with houses so scarce after the war
　　Stretching all along the river bank they were never an eyesore.
Living in the houseboats on the North Street river bank were good people
　　Virtually all of them as straight as the Parish Church steeple.
North Street with its long history had some good old Stanground names
　　And the people who lived there could hardly be described as vain.
They were most hard working, sincere and extremely generous to a fault
　　If it was their turn to buy a round of beer they wouldn't just bolt.
I must now dig deep in the grey matter to find names from earlier days
　　Names never used for years as I must write down without delay.
North Street has been the homes of the Ayres, the Smiths and Anthony's
　　Household names along with the Lees, the Sayers and Jacksons.
How could I possibly forget the Binghams, the Craythornes and Bakers
　　And to my knowledge no-one was missing from that bomb crater.
I delve even deeper and I find the Brewsters, the Woolleys and Porters
　　The Woolleys were lovely and that includes their good-looking daughters.
My memory is confused as I nearly forget the Hughes and even more Bakers
　　And still the names surface with the Dirlings, the Keens but not a Quaker.
Swirling around in my brain there comes to me the Sentances and Stallabrass
　　If I'd forgotten that name I definitely would be missing out on my past.
I have a rush of blood thinking of the Aldwinkle's, the Burbage's and Tanners
　　And the Tinkler's, the Wilmot's and the Taylor's, but never a Spanner.
The memory is now on overtime and still unfinished there comes a Cannon
　　It's such a long time since I've seen any Cannons, not even in spasms.
A Mr & Mrs Evans kept "The Woolpack" with the other pubs now all gone
　　I'm sure the regulars of "The Ferryboat" and "Anchor" had a swan song.
Opposite "The Woolpack" there lives a retired milkman of many years
　　He's been supping his beer there sixty years amongst the cheers.
With all the beer he's downed he's hardly likely to stop his drinking now
　　As an ex-milkman he enjoys his pint far more than milking a cow.

SCRUMPING AND CONKERS

Scrumping apples was an occasional pastime from the orchard nearby
    I won't say where it was as I might be accused of a lie.
Some good apples they were but most were seen to be rotting on the ground.
    So the many apples we took they were simply lying around
I hope it does not seem that I was nothing more than a thieving little git
    But in those days with other boys it was all done with wit.
For me to go scrumping in Stanground was very much a part of growing up
    While eating those sweet apples amongst the buttercups.
We would go blackberry picking in different fields down Church Lane
    And on hot summer days to eat blackberries was our gain.
Another pastime which us boys always spent was climbing the highest trees
    The trees in the fields were there to climb and catch the breeze.
I think the lovely thing about being young is that there's hardly any fear
    Because it was great to be sitting on the top branch in the clear.
Do kids today get the buzz and challenge of climbing such high trees
    I'm afraid it would be boring so it obviously wouldn't please.
Throwing stones at the conker trees was such an exciting thing to do
    So when the conkers came tumbling down it was more than a few.
The two conker trees near the vicarage took one hell of a bashing
    Passers-by had to duck as branches and conkers came down crashing.
Then it was time to play conker games with a conker on the end of a string
    A conker game with other boys could be a thrilling thing.
And if one smashed an opponent's conker to bits that felt just fine
    And to damage nine other boys' conkers felt like champion time.
So a boy with an undamaged conker might feel like a King for a whole day
    Until someone else came along and took that feeling away.

South Street looks north with 'The Carpenters Arms' on the left and Coneygree Road opposite

The old Police Station in South Street, opposite Church Street, it stood for law and order says the author

Looking east along Coneygree Road

The Police Station on the left with High Street facing west towards Fletton

Looking west to High Street and Fletton before the Parkway arrived

*Looking west from Stanground at all the brickyard chimneys, when the London Brick
Company was a thriving industry*

Two more lost of the magnificent seven that was

One was 'The Bluebell' in South Street, now a private house

'The Coach and Horses' in High Street looking west recently closed

THE POSH

It would be about 1946 when I first started to support The Posh
    I'd go by the fields to Fletton hoping we wouldn't suffer a loss.
On that walk the excitement multiplied every step of the way
    How very blessed I was to be watching my team play.
With other lads I would see first team matches and reserves too
    The thrill of watching The Posh was too good to be true.
Not that they were a good side because they were quite ordinary
    But just to be there for us kids felt quite extraordinary.
To see them play was my delight, and I'd only miss a game if sick
    How posh they looked in their dazzling blue and white strip.
There was much hero worship of certain players like there is today
    Sometimes we would travel to see our heroes play away.
The London Road ground I thought must be the best ground in the land
    To come to that conclusion, I must have had my head in the sand.
But I'd rarely seen other grounds so Posh's ground was my Wembley
    And the atmosphere was so incredibly warm and friendly.
Arriving home afterwards we would play soccer against the church wall
    Our heroes came to life as we couldn't get enough of the ball.
Peterborough United on a Saturday was very much a part of growing up
    And if they managed to win some games they might win the cup.
Now all those years later I'm somewhat disillusioned with the game
    For me soccer has altered so much it's only the same in name.
The smaller clubs like Posh will continually struggle to even exist.
    Yet the Manchester Uniteds of this world become more elitist.
Top soccer is hardly a sport anymore but an astronomical business
    Being spoilt by millionaire players with huge greediness.
Oh for those 1946 Midland League days when I supported the Posh
    Sixpence would get me in the ground and have some left for nosh.

UNWELCOME VISITORS

At the rear of my Father's butchers shop was his long narrow yard
    And he had to tackle a massive problem or he'd be scarred.
Being a butcher he sold the finest meat and was well aware of hygiene
    Above all else he was most conscious of his shop being clean.
At the bottom of his yard there was The Lode which was a dyke really
    It meant that houses also that side of the street saw The Lode clearly.
Not only were the residents in their houses aware of rats, but my Dad also
    He just couldn't allow vermin in his yard so the rats had to go.
He then allowed about a dozen stray cats to roam at the rear of his yard
    This unpleasant problem was solved with the cats on full guard.
I can remember those cats coming up the yard wanting something to eat
    My Dad so grateful to the cats would feed them bits of raw meat.
Now just occasionally the rats would escape the cats guarding The Lode
    They might venture into people's houses as rats have no code.
One went up the stairs in our house and got into my parents' bedroom once
    Michael on seeing it fell down the stairs with a mighty bump.
Rats always frightened me and on growing up in Church Street I saw plenty
    I was sent to the coal shed once when the coalscuttle was empty.
While picking up the coal in the dark shed I did indeed feel fur in my hand
    With the loudest shout I dived out of that shed to safer land.
My hand couldn't stop shaking for months on end after that expedition
    Scared to go there again I wanted no repeat of that exhibition.
If I close my eyes even now many years later I can nearly feel that rat
    And then my Dad went rat catching and put an end to that.
Dad chased the rat all over the lawn with a big stick the next day
    Oh what a lovely Father as he put that rat away.

A NOMADIC LIFE

According to the English dictionary gypsies lead a nomadic life
    The wanderers are those who move when the time is right.
They lived in horse-drawn caravans in the leg-o-mutton field
    Not for them the conventional life as they refused to yield.
The leg-o-mutton so named as it really was the shape of a field
    With the shape of a mutton-o-leg being so well revealed.
For centuries gypsies the world over would regularly be on the move
    They couldn't settle anywhere as they refused to be subdued.
There would be much travelling for all gypsy families once upon a time
    Whether they move about the same way now is hard to define.
Occasionally a whole new family would move into the leg-o-mutton
    They might stay for a year but move at the press of a button.
With being on the move some of the children didn't have an education
    Simply because they were never settled in a regular location.
The local ones living in the leg-o-mutton were much more settled
    To my knowledge there being no racial abuse and not heckled.
To walk through the leg-o-mutton it joined up to Coneygree Road
    And there would be more gypsies there living in their abode.
I always got on well with them, with so many of the kids my friends
    They played sports like the rest of us pleasing me no end.
Gypsies evidently migrated from Northern India in the 9th century
    And settled in many countries but not always contentedly.
But they were such colourful characters who were harmless really
    Until they thought they were being picked on then it was scary.
It was well known locally that if annoyed they could be a tough lot
    The men had rugged good looks and muscles to match on top.
Then one of my family fell out with a big gypsy lad called Smith
    I wished I hadn't witnessed it as my brother refused to quit.

THE LEG-O-MUTTON FIST FIGHT

The bare-knuckle fistfight is just another incident not quite forgotten
    It involved two bare-chested young men but I felt rotten.
This incident was very much the talking point at Chapel Street School
    Which my brother would agree left him looking rather a fool.
One lunchtime a knock on the door informed Michael he was wanted
    He obviously knew he was in trouble and wasn't to be hunted.
Off he went for his appointment with the well-built John Smith
    The venue was the leg-o-mutton field and it wasn't a tiff.
Out of curiosity I followed my brother quite happily to the leg-o-mutton
    Followed by dozens of school kids who were not to be forgotten.
I then realized this would be a fistfight and a large crowd was there
    Michael the character of our family was doing it for a dare.
A big circle was formed for these two young fighters to enter the ring
    Michael's face said it all as I'm sure he thought he couldn't win.
Now a fistfight is a raw and really dangerous game with no referee
    Michael got such a beating that day that he could hardly see.
It's no exaggeration to say he was battered to the ground many times
    The punishment so ferocious to stop the fight would be kind.
Being eleven years old and quite upset I so desperately wanted him to win
    But it was so one-sided amid such a noisy unwelcome din.
At each knock down his friends were begging him to give up the fight
    "Stay down Mick" they shouted as he looked deathly white.
Eventually he did stay down which was much to everyone's relief
    All I can remember is being full of emotion and awful grief.
Of course I am not blaming my brother's burly opponent whatever
    Michael knew what could happen so maybe he was too clever.
For me to witness something so savage made my brother a hero that day
    And fighting death four years ago his courage would not go away.

THE FLOODS

My brain constantly working it's hardly a surprise what comes next
    Memories lying dormant for years felt as though I'd slept.
But I was reminded of what actually happened by a lady recently
    Don't forget to mention the floods she had said quite reasonably.
The floods around Stanground is of special interest for me to write down
    As I can remember 1947 clearly and fortunately no-one drowned.
That Winter had been most unusual in view of its severe harshness
    With endless weeks of snow and ice creating much hardship.
Sometimes people couldn't get out of their houses because of the snow
    Pretty as a picture everywhere and a real Christmas card show.
The snow finally melted in mid March with tons of water left galore
    And water escalating as massive flooding appeared from the thaw.
This devastating flooding over the landscape cut Stanground from Fletton
    Which meant scores of local people starting to get a sweat on.
The fields and the main road between the villages was flooded completely
    With some Stanground folk unable to get to work too easily.
Because of the extensive flooding one of the ways to Fletton was by boat
    As small and large boats were laid on and being pulled by a rope.
The rope stretched from the jetty in Church Street to Fletton's Glen
    Probably a quarter of a mile the floods would be from end to end.
I can remember some big lorries managing to get their way through
    But occasionally some vehicles got stuck with often more than two.
I'm sure the floods stayed for about three weeks which seemed endlessly
    With pals and myself cadging a ride on a boat smiling excessively.

THE KNOTHOLES

The river because of the floods overflowed its banks like elsewhere
    To see streets flooding fast caused many a man to swear.
Many fields around Stanground are situated on very low ground
    So it was not difficult to understand there was water around.
Stanground spilling over with floods could have become an island quickly
    Being nearly surrounded by water and raining incessantly.
Right across the landscape there were floods with the Knotholes overflowing
    Water rushing everywhere and the deluge still growing.
The Knotholes as they were called have been there years and full of water
    But the rising floods meant the water was not on a saunter.
Some Knotholes were extremely large pits which were minus the clay
    So the pits filled with water once the clay was taken away.
The clay from those Knotholes was taken to the brick company brickyards
    With millions of bricks over the years being made in those yards.
Those brick company Knotholes have certainly been there all my lifetime
    And I can well remember many local fishermen casting a line.
Always brimful of water they were in the area of Stanground and Fletton
    So to run around those old pits was something my Mum wasn't keen on.
I suppose it was dangerous for kids to play there as swimming was banned
    Those Knotholes were deep, but I thought to swim there would be grand.
There is still today I believe a boating club which uses a Knothole regularly
    That's good news because those old pits have been used sparingly.
With Peterborough being an expanding city much housing is now built
    I hope the planners of this housing programme will not feel guilt.
I've mentioned this because buildings are being built on old Knothole sites
    I presume the powers that be who pass such plans have got it right.

THE ITALIAN JOB

The brickyards were so much a part of Stanground when I was a boy
 Many Stanground men worked there, as their hands became sore.
In Fletton and Woodston the brickyard chimneys reached for the sky
 There being dozens of these chimneys which were so high.
Looking West and South from Stanground one could see quite a few
 Standing upright and proud they looked like in a queue.
The chimneys had to be high in order to transfer all that smoke away
 The smoke from the kilns burned the bricks that were made of clay.
It was a thriving industry and was owned by the London Brick Company
 And as one of Peterborough's biggest employers did bring security.
The men who stacked the clay bricks in the kilns had big strong hands
 Some workers stacking the bricks came from foreign lands.
It was tough sweaty work and many nationalities worked in those yards
 As the Italians stacked the bricks without making it look hard.
When the bricks were made they were stacked on lorries for transportation
 With the lorries delivering the bricks to various destinations.
It was thought that the majority of men in the brickyards were Italians
 Who settled in England after the war to become good citizens.
When captured in the war they became prisoners at a Yaxley prison camp
 I'm not sure how long they were imprisoned as spirits may have sank.
After the war living locally many brought over from Italy their families
 Who seemed to have settled in the community most admirably.
The Italian job of stacking those bricks has now virtually disappeared
 All but one yard is left and with the chimneys gone it's weird.

STANGROUND SPORTS C.C.

Cricket on the village green is often as compatible as fruit and cream
    And in the Summer among the leafy trees a game is to be seen.
That game years ago might well have taken place in Stanground
    Because in the distance was that familiar bat and ball sound.
After the war Stanground Sports would draw many people to see them play
    With many sitting on the boundary with their picnics on the day.
It would be 1946 when cricket clubs resumed play just after the war
    And Stanground people being well pleased with what they saw.
Stanground Sports as it was known then was always my Cricket Club
    This was the team I supported with passion, and they were good.
During my growing up years the club played on three different grounds
    And wherever they played I invariably followed them around.
One of those grounds was the field at the rear of my Father's shop
    I would be in my element there until the game had stopped.
With the sun shining all day this was English village cricket at its best
    And Stanground Sports for a few years had unlimited success.
The Club actually won the Peterborough Cricket League in 1946 and 47
    Add to that the Jaidka Cup and I was in seventh heaven.
It was in this village cricket atmosphere that I started at an early age
    With my Stanground cricket heroes being my regular craze.
Like most things in my memory I can fortunately recall the players' names
    Practically all of them played football and shone at both games.
We even had two of my heroes from Peterborough United in the team
    So Cliff Woods and Des Farrow made the Club stronger it seemed.
My favourite player was the opening batsman and skipper Tom Wright
    And to see him hit sixes into The Lode was my obvious delight.
Watching village cricket was the ideal preparation for me to play the game
    My enthusiasm started with Stanground Sports to my eternal gain.

Two of the Knothols facing north and west

The Great Floods of 1947, with Stanground cut off from Fletton. The only way to get to each village was by boat. The author remembers cadging a lift on this boat

The Black Bridge facing south across the River Nene. Fire damaged in the 60s caused this railway bridge to come down, now replaced by another bridge

AROUND THE FIREPLACE

Bodies huddled around the kitchen fireplace trying to keep warm
    It's the depths of winter outside as someone starts to yawn.
Like others in those days no-one would have heard of central heating
    So families would sit around the fire on makeshift seating.
With endless hands stretched out over the fire to feel the heat
    On shivering Winter evenings warming one's cold feet.
My family is spread around that log fire with much to talk about
    So much talking going on that sometimes one would shout.
Many subjects were spoken about with butchering one conversation
    My Dad wishing his butchers shop was in a better location.
That open kitchen log fire had a glow that was so ideal for toast
    With all those fast growing boys I wonder who ate the most.
When the fire was getting low someone had to fill the coalscuttle
    Thinking about that rat in the coal shed I wasn't going to hustle.
To hear the news on the wireless my Dad would expect us to be quiet
    He could then sit back in his chair while puffing his pipe.
I can't remember too many volunteers offering to make a cup of tea
    If one left one's seat it was soon taken, and that includes a wee.
The kitchen was quite ordinary with no wall-to-wall carpets like today
    With colour TV, videos and DVD's being umpteen years away.
With the kitchen being full of people there was also a cat and a dog
    And they were not moving either as the fire they would hog.
Yet as I look back that kitchen was such a loving and secure place
    I was in that snug and happy environment with many a joyous face.
There were odd arguments which would break out in that kitchen
    Michael often the culprit was told he'd just got to listen.
I'm sure in that kitchen I learned a lot and it was a real education
    And when Tony returned from India his tales were a revelation.

ICE BOXES

The reason people gathered around the fire was the lack of heating
    As families would crouch by the fire to keep warm while eating.
Society now is soft in comparison to parents' and grandparents' past
    So with no central heating then, bedrooms would freeze fast.
Youngsters of today have no idea how frightfully cold Winters were
    With customary snow and freezing ice causing quite a stir.
It's true that when I was a boy Winters then were definitely more severe
    As icy temperatures in some homes would really bring fear.
The water pipes in many homes would be frozen solid because of the ice
    Bedrooms in particular were really arctic places and not nice.
Windows would be completely frozen not only outside but also inside
    They really were ice boxes as under the blankets one would dive.
Heaven knows how many blankets and eiderdowns were used to keep warm
    Being so terribly heavy on the bed one couldn't move till dawn.
Going to the toilet in the night was a real effort to leave a warm bed
    But one had to move eventually or face the consequences instead.
I always had the problem of keeping my nose and ears warm at night
    To have a frozen nose wasn't funny as I must have looked a sight.
I thought my Father's refrigerator where he kept his meat was a cold place
    But bedrooms with such temperatures meant I always had a cold face.
To crawl out of bed in the mornings was hardly an enthusiastic cause
    Beds were as warm as toast as one struggled out on all fours.
I'm sure Eskimos would love the cold bedrooms just like their igloos
    But cold bedrooms have disappeared so I won't be singing the blues.

COULD DO BETTER

Trudging to school in the snow is something I can so well remember
    When years ago Winters started early, soon after September.
It's a fact Winters were then more severe than those we get today
    With much snow in Winters but brilliant Summers starting in May.
Often one was soaked through when finally arriving cold at the school
    To get hit by a snowball on the back of the neck felt really cool.
Some of the names in that school are still clear after all those early years
    I remember things from schooldays, but more recent it's not clear.
With pals who lived near me, we always walked to the school together
    Whatever mischief we got up to we made it regardless of the weather.
It's the schoolteachers though that stick out in my mind the most
    Headmaster, Mr Kingston, frightened me as much as any ghost.
He had a definite stern look about him and rarely seemed to smile
    And whenever I saw him I wouldn't smile for a while.
There was a rumour that to install discipline he used the dreaded rope
    So to get six strokes across the backside was certainly no joke.
Mr Kingston's sister Polly was also a teacher who physically used a ruler
    And six across the knuckles hurt like hell, she being a regular abuser.
Mrs Jones, a well respected teacher, always kept a classroom on its toes
    As Johnny Wollard, a teacher, lost control as pupils added to his woes.
Not forgetting sports-mad Tom Nutt, that makes five teachers in all
    There were others but after so many years that's all I can recall.
At this particular time any school report I had usually came by letter
    My parents must have been exasperated when it said "could do better".
I knew I would achieve nothing if I didn't apply a different attitude
    To have passed the 11+ I'd have shown my parents some gratitude.
By this time I was nearly 12 years old so I had got to apply myself more
    The overwhelming problem was I found classwork a crashing bore.

TOM NUTT

There was a School Teacher at Chapel Street School I must mention
 As this Sports Master undoubtedly deserves my full attention.
His name was Tom Nutt and sports-mad boys thought the world of him
 He installed the discipline in us for playing sports and to win.
We hadn't achieved much with cricket or football until he arrived
 All at once we started winning matches rather than just survive.
He was a good Sports Master and took an interest in whoever we were
 We developed as a team with his knowledge being the added spur.
Particularly at cricket the school team started winning some cups
 Once we had got that winning feeling we were not giving that up.
Tom Nutt was a teacher who was quite prepared to give something back
 He dedicated hours to school sports which before was slack.
I'm sure he's loved cricket and football with unrelented emotion
 He's had a lifetime interest in these sports with much devotion.
He has shown equal enthusiasm when coaching both these sports
 All youngsters were lucky because what he had couldn't be bought.
He also excelled as the Football Manager of the Peterborough Boys
 So the hours of work he put into his teams was such a good cause.
Peterborough Boys under his management were so often in the news
 His teams progressed rapidly having won more games than lose.
I'm sure many schools throughout Britain could now do with a Tom Nutt
 But it saddens me that many school sports fields are now shut.
The sale of school playing fields has been allowed to prosper for years
 As this politically correct attitude nearly reduces me to tears.
We are told that schools with traditional sports days are now past
 So what happens to the Tom Nutts of this world, could he be the last?
But many Peterborough boys have over the years much to thank Tom for
 Without the likes of him sports would be poorer of that I'm sure.

THE THREE JOHNS

Maybe I've played too much sport but the joy I've had is immeasurable
    To have made it big time my delight would be considerable.
With hindsight we can all look back on life to what might have been
    Hardly an academic I exerted my pleasure in a sports team.
My life though couldn't have been better and honestly I've no regrets
    And when I was young I played all sports with enthusiastic effect.
So if I was disappointed somewhat that I just didn't progress at sport
    Others more talented would be more disappointed I'd have thought.
I name three Johns who if they had been born at a different time
    Might well now be tasting the fruits of more than just wine.
These three Stanground born boys I thought had above average ability
    Perhaps they lacked a certain something that creates stability.
Youngsters can have obvious talent but perhaps luck plays a part in sport
    Some may progress further and it's not always the one you thought.
But these three Johns who all about my age, anything was probable
    Another time, another place, it might just have been possible.

John Craythorne's name brings schoolboy cricket memories back
    He was a really outstanding cricketer who couldn't half bat.
We were in the same Stanground school cricket and soccer teams together
    A natural sportsman his superiority shone in any weather.
In summer playing cricket he would hit the ball like a shot from a rifle
    The ball went such a long way it was best to retrieve it by cycle.
A really good-looking left-handed batsman who took some dislodging
    If he wanted to, he would definitely stay for board and lodging.
I only saw one schoolboy cricketer better and that's not said in jest
    As this boy became England's Cricket Captain, so he was the best
Such high praise indeed because John Craythorne was so exceptional
    And what he achieved later in Club Cricket was quite remarkable.
We have played against each other many times since those school days
    But he's well retired from cricket now and amended his ways.
How he never made a professional cricketer, I'll never honestly know
    He had wonderful talent which really should have been on show.

THE THREE JOHNS continued

Like so many kids in Winter, I was soccer mad when I was young
With my pal Johnny Rose it was always such immense fun.
He lived round the corner from me and we practised for hours on end
And just like Beckham of today we really tried to make it bend.
We played near the conker trees and in a field down Church Lane
As we dribbled, passed and headed that ball again and again.
John went to school in Fletton where his skilfulness was put to the test
He proved himself in schools soccer as definitely one of the best.
A better player than me he was always a regular for Peterborough Boys
And with the ball at his feet he controlled it like a precious toy.
He should have progressed much further as he didn't have feet of clay
The last I ever heard of him he had emigrated to the U.S.A.

John Steels when he punched your lights out he carried quite a sting
As this John more than exceeded himself in the boxing ring.
A real tough boy and no one ever dared pick a fight with him
And if they ever did they would find themselves out on a limb.
I went with him for boxing training in Peterborough at the Triangle Pub
I received quite a few hammerings there and felt like a cub.
He had a big punch like horses hooves and had undoubted class
With his swift movements round the ring making him quite fast.
It would be about five years ago I last saw him on the bowling green
He hadn't altered much from when I last saw him in his teens.
I think he was too much of a gentleman to be a committed fighter
All I know is that when he punched me I felt a stone lighter.

THE MAGNIFICENT SEVEN

There were seven pubs in Stanground and were not known as magnificent
  But surely seven pubs in the thirties and forties was sufficient.
I find it remarkable that small villages in the past had so many pubs
  Even more remarkable they survived without selling pub grub.
Ask a landlord today and he'd say if he didn't sell food he wouldn't exist
  So to rely totally on the sale of just beer his business is at risk.
They must have been a real thirsty lot living South of the River Nene
  With those pubs partly full of people, but not a woman to be seen.
Those were the days when women were not always seen in public houses
  Also in those days some men wouldn't enter a pub with their spouses.
A woman either married or single would hardly enter a pub on her own
  As her place in those days if she was married would be in the home.
Now whether the seven pubs were magnificent it's difficult to say
  But years ago when times were tough, that pint would go a long way.
In North Street there was "The Anchor", "The Ferryboat" and "The Woolpack"
  Today only "The Woolpack" remains as the others have had the sack.
"The Golden Lion" in Church Street is the pub I've already spoken about
  Its regulars might call at the fish shop and in good voice no doubt.
Opposite Coneygree Road and in South Street is "The Carpenters Arms"
  Next door was another fish shop which may have added to its charms.
South Street was the home of a thatched roof pub called "The Bluebell"
  Evidently it was the best beer locally so regulars would tell.
Being the oldest pub in the village it's been closed now for some time
  It's now rather a quaint little cottage and it's aged like good wine.
In High Street on the way to Fletton there's "The Coach and Horses"
  Recently closed it's always raised money for many good causes.
I now think those pubs were the magnificent seven and some survived
  They were part of Stanground's heritage with three still alive.

BIG MICK

My brother Michael with his schooling was even less of a scholar than me
  I'm convinced he tried his hardest, though it just wasn't to be.
Years ago while growing up Michael seemed constantly to be in trouble
  And with Michael's trouble he always found it at the double.
He might occasionally arrive home from school with a red bloody nose
  Mum realising he'd been in a fight, it only added to her woes.
In his middle teens for a bet he took on a professional boxer in the ring
  The Bridge Fair was in town so this fight was the real thing.
He had to stay on his feet for the whole of three rounds to earn £5
  Evidently he did just that, but he was savagely knocked around.
With pals cheering him on he somehow managed to stay on his feet
  So with the fight over it would be a long walk home to Church Street.
Arriving home he told Mum he had fallen over and his face was a mess
  He'd tell his Mother anything as most things were said in jest.
In his early life anything could happen to him being so very injury prone
  He fell from a moving car once and luckily never broke a bone.
He would hilariously ride his cycle backwards looking over his shoulder
  He was a good circus act sitting on handlebars as he got bolder.
At fourteen he went to Peterborough Cattle Market and bought a goat
  Walking the goat in town he saw Mum and said he'd got it for nowt.
I suppose my parents' three other boys were boring in comparison to Michael
  He'd give anything a try once which always added to the sparkle.
With Michael being five years older than me I was often called Young Mick
  That name stuck with me for years but no way did I have his wit.
A bachelor he lived his life with Mum and nursed her for three long years
  And so lovingly looked after her that he may have had a few tears.
Because of his personality and huge frame everyone would know Big Mick
  I'm still coming to terms with his death, a brother I'll never forget.
I like to think he's reunited with his parents where we all might go one day
  Perhaps he's making his presence felt in that place far away.

FURTHER DISTRACTIONS

Yes I was probably twelve years old when something else took my fancy
   The opposite sex had entered my life and her name wasn't Nancy.
On approaching my teens I was well aware this was a natural occurrence
   Stanground was full of pretty girls so I had to be more observant.
This was something entirely different from all the games I'd ever played
   I'd found a new pastime and it wasn't to be any further delayed.
All of a sudden Chapel Street School was a very exciting place for me to be
   Looking forward to school was a whole new ball game experience for me.
I hardly needed any further diversion because of this most recent attraction
   My schoolwork had suffered enough without any further distraction.
My Mother I know didn't appreciate my sudden interest in the opposite sex
   As she thought I'd bring shame to the family by what comes next.
Growing up in those days wasn't easy as parents never told their kids a thing
   As regards myself I was shy and didn't know much about anything.
Any talk in our house about sex would make my Mother feel uncomfortable
   The subject was rarely raised and my Mother's relief was considerable.

Heroes

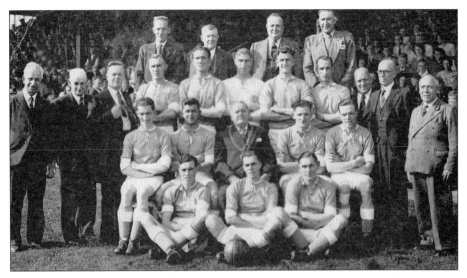

Peterborough United (The Posh) 1946-47
The author still remembers all the players names, heroes are never forgotten

Stanground Sports C.C. 1946

L to R: S. Croxford, J. Harvey, R. Cuffe, E. Aveling, R. Dunkley, F. Fairchild, G. Cameron, C. Church, R. Rippon, J. Croxford, S. Twelvtree.
D. Blewit, D. Farrow, T. Wright, M. Wells, J. Polhill, C. Woods, A. Bains.
With their president the Rev. Morley Wells, photograph taken at the rear of the vicarage. The author rates this team the best local side in Peterborough at the time. Tom Wright the skipper is left of Rev. Wells

The all conquering Chapel Street School Cricket Team 1947

Chapel Street School Cricket Team 1947 (three cups won that season)
Back Row (L to R): T Nutt (Sports Master), Unknown, P Kingston (Headmaster),
Unknown, V Jackson
3rd Row (L to R): D Strangwood, B Tinkler, K Keen
2nd Row (L to R): B Holdich, R Woods, M Sayers, J Craythorne (Captain),
T Moulds, V Jackson, R Elderkin
Front Row (L to R): T Baker, P Hughes

The Chapel Street School Football Team 1947
Back Row (L to R): P Kingston (Headmaster), B Holdich, J Woollard (Teacher)
Middle Row (L to R): R Elderkin, B Tinkler, S Baker, V Jackson,
T Tyers, C Pepper,
Front Row (L to R): J Craythorne (Captain), T Baker, M Sayers, R Woods, T Moulds

A MOMENTOUS DECISION

I was twelve years old when my parents made a momentous decision
    My schoolwork needed improvement and more supervision.
It was decided I should attend as a day student at Stamford School
    I was excited one minute and the next decisively cool.
My parents were giving me the opportunity of a public school education
    With my failure at school so far it hardly felt a celebration.
There really was much sadness as I'd be leaving my old school mates
    I was upset that I would never again walk through those school gates.
I'd be catching two coaches for the journey to Stamford of fourteen miles
    So I really did think I'd be travelling well into the wilds.
Being at public school I would be mixing with sons of professional people
    It was imperative therefore to be strong and not seen as feeble.
How would an ordinary boy from Stanground village ever be accepted
    Or to put another way, what would I have to do to be respected.
I knew that in comparison Stamford School was not an Eton or Harrow
    But would I find snobbishness there making me feel shallow?
I honestly didn't know what to expect being in this new environment
    And just how would it affect my whole future development?
These were the unanswered questions which would soon be answered
    As I began to look upon this new school as something ventured.
With failing the Eleven Plus this was my chance of the best education
    Being so privileged this would hopefully be my realization.

STAMFORD SCHOOL

Stamford School was founded by a William Radcliffe in the year 1532
    Thousands of pupils have passed through the school, not just a few.
The Georgian town of Stamford stands on the banks of the River Welland
    And it's situated at the very heart of peaceful middle England.
The school still stands on its original site close to the town centre
    With its many up-to-date facilities and splendid extensions.
During the last century it experienced much growth and development
    Now hundreds of pupils study at the school in a good environment.
Over the years the school has built up a fine reputation and traditions
    With so many pupils fulfilling their long-standing ambitions.
The school is known for its academic standards and educational activities
    To be fortunate to be educated there produces endless possibilities.
Stamford in 1947 was an historic market town of about 14,000 people
    Depending on one's approach one can see many church steeples.
It has often been described as a most beautiful and interesting town
    And even before the Roman Conquest traces of man were found.
The centre of the town still retains many fine and original buildings
    With its medieval layout and numerous unique attractions.
Its great history has attracted many thousands of visitors every year
    As the tourists explore into its ancient history of yesteryear.
It lies in South Lincolnshire with its excellent and quite elegant views
    And on the thriving market day there may even be queues.
This then was the town I'd be travelling daily to further my education
    But attending this elite posh school I was full of trepidation.

THE STANGROUND BOY AT STAMFORD SCHOOL

So the Stanground boy set off for his new school in some anticipation
   With my parents full of hope and rightful expectation.
The coach trip in the early days to Stamford felt like a hundred miles
   As school children wore blazers and caps dressed to the nines.
Those first few weeks were so active with the travelling and the new school
   My feet hardly touched the ground as I tried to stay cool.
Arriving by coach at Stamford it was often a mad dash to the chapel
   Sometimes moving so quickly like escaping a rugby tackle.
Being a religious school, every morning there was a service for $\frac{1}{4}$ of an hour
   Then it was off to the classrooms where the masters would wield power.
It was enough for me to learn English without the hassle of Latin and French
   I must admit to missing my old school which was proving a wrench.
Being optimistic I tried to give my schoolwork its utmost attention
   But I was struggling to cope and loaded down with apprehension.
My schoolwork, the discipline and the punishment beatings were hard to take
   And with all that homework was just too much for heaven's sake.
The homework was an absolute nightmare and I didn't really have a clue
   But I wasn't the only none too bright one as there were a few.
It was on the morning coach that classmates helped with my homework
   Then we would copy each other's to prove we hadn't shirked.
I did form great friendships there otherwise I wouldn't have coped so well
   Because without those classmates it could have been sheer hell.
The fear of any snobbery and not being accepted never really did occur
   Sometimes I would enjoy the school with sport the added spur.
I also knew that boys at public schools are subjected to being bullied
   I never did experience any at the school so I was hardly worried.
But my work in class had deteriorated alarmingly and was quite pathetic
   So when the headmaster sent for me he was not sympathetic.

PUNISHMENT

At the school I found similarities with the novel Tom Brown's Schooldays
    As I was to experience corporal punishment to amend my ways.
On approaching the Headmaster's study I was nervous and feared the worse
    Why had I from the whole of the school been singled out for the birch?
The Headmaster spoke for ten minutes that my schoolwork must get better
    He then ordered me to remove my blazer and school sweater.
Shaking with fear I bent down with each hand gripping the arms of a chair
    I should really have been grateful that my bottom wasn't bare.
After three strikes with his stick across my backside I couldn't take any more
    So I stood up with tears in my eyes with my bottom scorching sore.
"Get down Holdich and take your punishment like a man," he then said
    Being in my early teens I never forgot those words and wished I were dead.
I well knew at this stage what poor Tom Brown went through at Rugby School
    How humiliating it was and I felt rather more than just a fool.
After six strikes I staggered out of his study with my buttocks on fire
    As with each stroke from the Headmaster he never seemed to tire.
For the Stanground boy as time went by the schoolwork became even tougher
    I was paying a high price for being such a complete and utter duffer.
Later I mentioned this beating to my Dad when he was in a good mood
    He replied, "You must have deserved it. So you must improve".
My Dad's answer was typical of what any Father would say at that time
    But I felt degraded and thought I'd committed some sort of crime.
I respected my Father too much to argue so what he said was just fine
    He had every right to be annoyed instead of being kind.

THE THREE HOUSES

When I first attended Stamford School one would be put to a house
    School House, Town House or Country House so one couldn't grouse.
With being an all male school the School educated well over 550 boys
    Whatever house one belonged to it gave a definite pride and joy.
School House with over 200 pupils would of course be all boarders
    Who would be permanently living in their school house quarters.
Town House was for all students who actually lived in Stamford Town
    This was by some way the smallest of the three houses to be found.
Country House with the largest number of pupils were country drawn
    Drawn from the areas outside of Stamford so were country born.
So as I came from Peterborough it was Country House I qualified for
    To be picked by one's house for sport one was proud as never before.
To represent any of the houses at sport it gave one immense felicity
    So whenever a house played each other there was intense rivalry.
It was at this school I learned the full value of sporting enjoyment
    Always play any game hard but fair, which then brings fulfilment.
If a game is lost offer congratulations which shouldn't be delayed
    And take defeat in a good spirit, above all else be well behaved.
I like to think I carried this through to my adult life whatever the game
    Whether win or lose my attitude would always be the same.
I've never been able to tolerate bad sportsmanship in sport of any sort
    Youngsters must be taught the correct attitude I'd have thought.
Everyone I'm sure likes to win at any game which one will partake
    So house matches played in the proper spirit were just great.

LOSING TOUCH

When a youngster moves from a village school problems may arise
    This had happened to me when I bade my old schoolmates goodbye.
Then school kids every year on passing the 11+ are in this situation
    The reason is they move from that friendly and solid foundation.
Some have probably never ventured further than their birthplace
    More so years ago when people didn't move about like today's race.
The constant travelling to Stamford and back each day was a bind
    As those old coaches were most uncomfortable for that daily grind.
With two coaches to catch home the journey put me under some pressure
    On arriving home each day at 6 pm I hardly had any leisure.
Having an evening meal and the wretched homework it was then to bed
    But I'd have preferred playing ball with the village lads instead.
So at home all sports were out for the evenings but not weekends
    So being able to play sports with the lads pleased me no end.
The fear was also that with old pals I could be gradually losing touch
    Friendships formed long ago and the very thought hurt me much.
I know that when I left Stamford School I picked up where I was before
    I renewed friendships as the thought of losing pals hurt me more.
While at Stamford School I was conscious of my public school education
    And not just because my parents were full of hope and expectation.
It was because I was living in Stanground and going to school elsewhere
    As old school friends on seeing my school uniform would stare.
To be honest I didn't want old friends to see me in my new school clothes
    As it was quite possible I may well have got under someone's nose.
I was so conscious that with a private education I was classed as elite
    Nothing would be further from the truth as old friends I'd greet.
I've never ever been able to tolerate class distinction in any form
    The class system encourages snobbery, but not where I was born.

Stamford School with the school Chapel on the right

The School Hall
80

Boxing training in the school Hall taken by the gym master Mr Wolvenden. Boxing of course is banned now at many schools, which includes Stamford School

M.J.K. Smith the authors' schoolboy hero goes on the attack playing cricket on the school cricket field

The author with two of the cricket and rugby teams he played for at Stamford School

School Under 14 XI., 1949
D.S. Mitchell, B.W. Holdich, N.J. Rowe, T.E. Lewin, R. Fisher, G.H. Hornby, D.J. Kinder
I. Hayes, C.W.R. Coggan, Esq., C.E. Doughty (Capt.), C.R. Smith, J. Dobbie

Country House Junior Rugger Cup 1949
R.G. Penford, B.J. Knowles, M.G. Grey, J.M. Simmons, K.E. Williamson, E. Brogan, R. Fisher, J.N. Cresswell
J.M. Plant, D.W. Bird, H.E. Packer Esq., W.G. Greenfield (Capt), C.W.R. Coggan Esq., R.E. Rudkin,
R.A. Robinson, J.A. Rimmington, B.W. Holdich

82

SOME SCHOOL MASTERS

Memories of some Stamford School masters I'm never likely to forget
   With Tom Brown's Schooldays evident as some scared me to death.
Rushing around in their long flowing black gowns and flat pointed hats
   One couldn't miss a master as they strode from class to class.
Some were so fierce looking I'm sure they had no sense of humour at all
   I remember thinking "Do these people smile at home" I can recall.
I'm sure that some masters I shall quite possibly remember forever
   For the simple reason some of them permanently had me in a tether.
To see them enter the classroom was enough to make me feel depressed
   There being always the constant fear of another six of the best.
At times because of my poor work in the class my confidence had sunk
   And with some of those masters I was hardly flavour of the month.
But there was humour in class when dear old Bruno Brown took a lesson
   And with this master we were in for a quite humorous session.
At times we played up unmercifully as Bruno invariably lost the plot
   How he tolerated us I don't know, but I knew we liked him a lot.
Latin lessons were great when for $\frac{1}{4}$ hour (Brag) Hughes talked rugby
   To hear Brag Hughes boasting about Welsh Rugby was lovely.
As for the Latin we encouraged this master to talk about anything else
   I didn't think anyone enjoyed Latin and that included the Welsh.
After some time he got the message and then it was back to the lesson
   We had to be satisfied as to get off Latin was such a blessing.
There was a Mr Wolfenden a former amateur boxer and the Gym master
   And as I was a boxer and showed promise he befriended me ever after.
For once at Stamford School I was indeed a favourite of some master at last
   "Alleluia" "Alleluia" as all the other masters had given up on the task.
Mr (Bill) Packer another master was a bit special and a class act
   I admired and looked up to him so very much and that's a fact.

SCHOOL PREFECTS ALSO

Another time I received corporal punishment was from a school prefect
    This beating so-called would hopefully have the desired effect.
School prefects in those days could give punishment which was violent
    So along with two other school friends I was to be silenced.
All of us came from Peterborough and we were very much best friends
    As I've mentioned before without friends it could have been the end.
I feel there's two such school friends here that I must mention at least
    As with John Stanyon and John Cresswell memories never cease.
We had all been reported for being too boisterous on the school coach
    Having received corporal punishment before I feared it the most.
The beatings were in the top dormitory which was known as School House
    We were then lectured by two prefects that we behaved like louts.
To walk to the top dormitory was to walk up several flights of stairs
    For me it felt like a hanging job and I was definitely most scared.
As I was the last one to climb those stairs my two pals returned in tears
    This hardly gave me any confidence amongst unparalled fears.
Because of the threat of libel I shall refer to them as Number 1 and Number 2
    And if they are alive today it just wouldn't be fair to name those two.
So here was I being described by Number 1 as a complete and utter hooligan
    The other one Number 2 was swishing his whipping stick on conclusion.
I was told to bend down which was fast becoming such a familiar position
    Number 2 I'd heard was strong in the arm so I was filled with suspicion.
He was eighteen years old and he inflicted more pain than the Headmaster
    "Why did I deserve beatings I thought" as each strike became faster.
I left that dormitory in severe pain with tears streaming down my face
    On realizing the punishment was harsh I had to accept my fate.
Seeing Number 2 from then on I eyed him suspiciously after that beating
    My backside was alight for days and felt like central heating.
With this Victorian style discipline I began to feel sorry for myself
    But I didn't dare tell my Dad this time as I valued my health.

MR (BILL) PACKER

My Country House Master was a Mr (Bill) Packer whom I shall not ignore
    He being a gentleman whom every sports mad boy would adore.
I was lucky that this legendary figure was my Country House Master
    I'd have gone through a brick wall for him and that's for starters.
It was said that (Bill) Packer only favoured a pupil if he played sport
    Well, I can't complain with that as my cricket and rugby he taught.
If Country House won any house cups his wife invited the team for tea
    Eating cream cakes and being spoilt was a new experience for me.
(Bill) Packer effectively made my time at the school more pleasurable
    His name synonymous with sport made my pleasure memorable.
He took me home once to Stanground in his car after I fell in the gym
    My Mum said he was a real gentleman and thought the world of him.
Evidently every boy he taught, a note was made in his little black book
    What he made of me I never knew but it would be worth a quick look.
Over thirty years later I saw him in Stamford and made myself known
    He looked at me in an old-fashioned way with much interest shown.
On telling him my name he was full of curiosity as he stroked his chin
    After all he'd last seen me as a boy when I was a skinny young thing.
He even remembered my initials and quite pleased I was doing well
    His memory was remarkable as once again I fell under his spell.
He gave extraordinary service to Stamford School and to the town
    Serving on various committees and where his ideas were so sound.
Among his achievements perhaps one stands out above others the most
    A young blond boy became a double international whom he'd coached.
Mr (Bill) Packer died in 1994 and this man was well loved and respected
    The funeral was full with mourners which was only to be expected.

SCHOOL SPORTS

If there was one subject I loved at Stamford School it was the sport
    With such a variety the school wasn't so bad after all I thought.
I must have made an impression and was soon in the school boxing team
    Any frustrations in class I got my own back in the ring it seemed.
Cricket, boxing, rugby, athletics and swimming I was spoilt for choice
    And not forgetting hockey and tennis if one wanted of course.
Being soccer mad I was disappointed to be told I must play the rugby game
    I didn't take to rugby at first so things weren't quite the same.
Rugby Union is traditionally a sport being played at all public schools
    But the more I played the game the less I thought it was for fools.
There's togetherness in rugby which is rarely found in the other sports
    Once I got the feel and understanding of the game I was caught.
When I see a Six Nations Championship game on TV I have a good look
    And the excitement the game generates I'm well and truly hooked.
Had I stayed longer at school I might have received School Colours for sport
    I would have been so proud but School Colours cannot be bought.
I look back on the sports I played at the school and can claim some success
    The school was wonderful for sport and I simply enjoyed the best.
It was worth attending Stamford School in view of the sports I played
    With those sports facilities being most emphatically displayed.
The School Cricket Pavilion was one of the best to be seen for miles
    And its thatched roof being seen as portraying a unique style.
The lush green grass of those playing fields were so very noticeable
    So to play sports there was for me and many others so beneficial.
How different for sports there from the Stanground recreation ground
    Because the Stamford School playing fields were the best around.
So privileged was I to be playing sports in such fine surroundings
    I've never forgotten I was lucky to have such a sports grounding.

M. J. K. (BLONDIE)

Through watching a school rugby match an inspiring new hero emerged
    This hero I could see most days, so such memories did occur.
He seemed everyone's hero and was affectionally known as Blondie
    So Michael John Knight Smith is always remembered fondly.
In cricket his brilliant batting occupied the crease most of the time
    And at rugby he was quite majestic and an undoubted find.
He was a marvellous games player and quite outstanding at hockey
    And in athletics whatever he did he was never, ever cocky.
Mike Smith was two years older than me and became a sports star
    To see this wonderful talent everyone knew he'd go really far.
With his blond hair he strode the sports field like an Olympian figure
    So on leaving school we knew he would achieve something bigger.
Playing cricket and rugby for England he was a Double International
    And to play two sports for your country is quite phenomenal.
He also became England's Cricket Captain and was known as M.J.K.
    These being his initials by which he still answers to today.
It was said he was a fine England Captain and that's said only about a few
    Because although he demanded respect he was really popular too.
"A man you would go in the jungle for" an England cricketer said of him
    So the chances of not getting along with him were very slim.
If you were looking for an Officer and a Gentleman it would be M.J.K.
    Being unselfish and scrupulously fair in any game he did play.
On seeing Mike Smith most days I was to witness a live sporting hero
    I even contemplated walking like him but in comparison I was zero.
For all his success evidently he hasn't changed from those years past
    You see, I pick my heroes carefully and I wanted mine to last.

APPOINTMENT WITH A HERO

Those few years at Stamford School I watched but never spoke to M.J.K.
  I was really in awe of him but always hoped we'd meet some day.
It was fifty-five years later that finally a meeting had been arranged
  So I was fairly confident that our meeting wouldn't be strained.
I met M.J.K. in the pavilion of the Northamptonshire County Cricket Club
  And this meeting proceeded to be everything I expected it would.
To meet a school hero from over fifty years ago can be a disappointment
  But I felt I knew the man so I was confident for this appointment.
I spent about $1\frac{1}{2}$ hours in his company one Friday in September 2004
  We talked about cricket, rugby and Stamford School for sure.
No wonder England cricketers had spoken of him with genuine affection
  As I couldn't have asked for more from his friendly reception.
He was most courteous and he increased his standing in my estimation
  So to be in the presence of such a man I had no reservations.
My abiding memory of M.J.K. was that he spoke with a certain authority
  And as a former England Cricket Captain showed no superiority.

LEAVING SCHOOL

My three years at Stamford School had ended for me most abruptly
    The Headmaster having written to my parents quite amicably.
He felt there was literally no point at all in my staying on at school
    So I was back to square one where I know life can be cruel.
I know I'd had many problems with my schoolwork being awful at least
    But I was in total shock that my Stamford School days had ceased.
The Headmaster had written courteously hoping I'd find a decent job
    My parents might well have thought at this stage I'd finish up a yob.
I knew I'd let my parents down dreadfully which left me depressed
    I had squandered a marvellous opportunity I must confess.
The advantage I'd had of a public school education left me ashamed
    And not for the first time in my young life I was to blame.
Looking back to that age of fifteen it was a definite low in my life
    Having that education and blowing it I was full of contrite.
I became shy in company and as for my personality I hadn't got one
    How could I be involved in conversation if I was seen as dumb?
I must admit that those three years at that school went quite quickly
    And even today thinking about corporal punishment I get jittery.
The grisly incident of prefects giving acute physical pain is well past
    Thank God this vile humiliation has now disappeared at last.
If I am critical of Stamford School it's not intentional in any way
    Remember, I've written as it was then, being so different today.
But I know in this modern time the school has a very good reputation
    So with corporal punishment now gone that's cause for celebration.
Things I'd miss most at the school would undoubtedly be all that sport
    If I'd been judged on sport my marks would be a different sort.
I won't be the first one who has disregarded a fantastic opportunity
    But I now humbly admit that I did fail rather conclusively.
As I left the school that Summer my brother Gordon started next term
    Seeing another Holdich it was enough to make the masters squirm.
But Gordon was a success deserving his high position later in the bank
    I was proud of his achievements at school, but I had drawn a blank.
Yet against much disappointment of being asked to leave that school
    I'm so proud to have been there, if only I hadn't been such a fool.

FIFTY-FIVE YEARS LATER

My story is now briefly brought up to date after nearly fifty-five years
 And I think I've been reasonably successful despite early fears.
On leaving school I obtained an apprenticeship as an electrical fitter
 I knew though it wasn't for me, but I've never been a quitter.
Going into the Army for two years National Service was my saviour
 And running up hills in Hong Kong in battle dress was hard labour.
I was called into the forces as a nineteen-year-old boy fearing the worse
 The Army made a man of me and sometimes made me curse.
My attitude changed and I saw out my time with renewed confidence
 To have completed my two years I was not an unhappy occupant.
Eventually after trying other jobs I then became an insurance man
 So I became "The man from the Pru" and I was as happy as a lamb.
I worked for the Prudential for thirty years and refound my self-esteem
 All those years of lost confidence I was a success it seemed.
My message then it's not the end of the world if one is a poor scholar
 One can be quite successful and still feel like a million dollars.
I've tried to be totally honest as I've laid bare my soul in this book
 It's surprised me that things long forgotten now have a new look.
At this moment the Stanground boy again thinks of his Mum and Dad
 So lucky to be born to them with the best parents one could have.
I believe to be born to a loving family my brothers and I had a good start
 My parents have been gone a few years but never escape my heart.
I think of Derek the evacuee who lived with my family in the war years
 We have been in touch again so surely that's worth a few beers.
I know I had problems at school but I now think my early life was idyllic
 And if I live to be a hundred years old I know I'll never forget it.
The older I get I think of a fireplace which the family would surround
 So I couldn't possibly ask for more having been born in Stanground.

EIPILOGUE (One Day To Live)

If I had one day to live I'd want to visit Stanground one last time
    Because the Stanground I've known, its memories are all mine.
To see the conker trees near the vicarage I'd want to throw stones
    I might well strike lucky with many conkers around my toes.
One last visit to the parish church I'd want to hear the bells ring
    Memory informs me of a wonderful choir who really could sing.
I might try to swim where the Black Bridge crosses the River Nene
    Can I be serious as I haven't been swimming there since my teens.
In the fields I'd think of Peter Fairchild, Ray Woods and John Rose
    We couldn't play sports though as we suffer with aching bones.
Seeing chapel Street School I'd think of the poverty and the war
    Undernourished kids with holes in their shoes, that's what I saw.
If I saw on the last day of my life an American car I'd think of Yanks
    Cruising around Stanground those cars were as big as any tank.
With crime today now out of control I think of the old village Bobby
    As this type of Bobby was so dedicated his job was nearly a hobby.
A final last look at High Street, Coneygree Road and South Street
    Also Mount Pleasant and North Street where old friends I'd greet.
The Raiders from Fletton might be about on their side of The Lode
    But at my age if stones were thrown I'd quickly want a commode.
The last day I might even think of the Boatyards and the Knotholes
    I definitely wouldn't have time for that last game of bowls.
I would also have to have one final look at the house where I was born
    With its thousands of memories I could break down and be forlorn.
I'd want a pint in one of the three pubs left of the Magnificent Seven
    Providing I didn't drink too much and think I was half way to Heaven.
Later I'd say to my family I'd seen Stanground for the very last time
    So now I think it's an appropriate time to finish with my rhymes.

Still good friends
A recent photograph of the author (left) with the former evacuee
Derek Bishop from London. Derek stayed with the Holdich
family for eight years. Considered at the time
one of the longest serving evacuee's ever